METABOLIC CONFUSION DIET COOKBOOK FOR ENDOMORPH WOMEN OVER 50

1000+ DAYS OF INGENIOUS CARB-CYCLING STRATEGIES FOR POWERFUL WEIGHT LOSS AND ENHANCED METABOLIC HEALTH | 56-DAY MEAL PLAN INCLUDED

JASMIN CHARLES

Copyright © 2024 by Jasmin Charles

SCAN THE QR CODE AND IMMEDIATELY ACCESS YOUR 3 SPECIAL BONUSES IN DIGITAL FORMAT!

🔥 **Bonus 1: Dining Out Without Derailing Your Diet**

🔥 **Bonus 2: Recognizing Your Body Type**

🔥 **Bonus 3: Weekly Grocery Planner**

TABLE OF CONTENTS

INTRODUCTION

Welcome to Your New Journey

Welcome to your new journey into the world of healthier living and sustained well-being through the Metabolic Confusion Diet, specifically tailored for endomorph women over the age of 50. This innovative approach to dieting is not just another trend; it's a scientifically grounded method designed to revitalize your metabolism and help you achieve weight loss in a sustainable manner.

Understanding the Metabolic Confusion Diet begins with recognizing its core principle: variability. Traditional diets often fail because they impose rigid, unchanging meal plans that our bodies adapt to over time. In response, the metabolic rate—the rate at which your body burns calories—can plateau or even decline, leading to frustrating weight loss stalls. The Metabolic Confusion Diet, however, continuously keeps your body guessing through strategic variations in carbohydrate and calorie intake. This variability can prevent metabolic adaptation, potentially increasing your overall metabolic rate and fat-burning capacity.

For endomorphs, typically characterized by a fuller figure and a propensity to store fat more easily than other body types, revving up the metabolism is crucial. After 50, this challenge is compounded by natural decreases in muscle mass and hormonal changes that can further slow the metabolic rate. By implementing a carb-cycling regimen, the Metabolic Confusion Diet directly addresses these challenges. It alternates between high-carb and low-carb days, not only to boost metabolism but also to support hormonal balance, enhance energy levels, and curb cravings.

But how exactly does this benefit you? On high-carb days, your body receives a signal to ramp up energy expenditure. You might feel more energetic and capable of handling more intense or longer-duration exercises, which are essential for muscle maintenance and boosting your metabolic rate. Conversely, on low-carb days, your body turns to stored fat for energy, which can lead to effective fat loss. This cycling thus supports weight loss while minimizing the loss of lean muscle mass, a common issue in many conventional diets that can lead to a sluggish metabolism.

Moreover, this diet isn't just about losing weight; it's about reshaping your relationship with food and eating patterns. It encourages you to listen to your body and eat intuitively—important as your nutritional needs and appetite can change significantly after the age of 50. By understanding and adapting to these needs, you're more likely to enjoy a range of foods and maintain a balanced diet, rich in nutrients needed to support ageing bodies, like calcium for bone health and antioxidants for cellular repair and maintenance.

Another significant advantage of the Metabolic Confusion Diet is its flexibility, which makes it particularly appealing and sustainable. Unlike strict diets that require meticulous calorie counting or restrictive food lists, this diet offers the freedom to adjust based on your personal preferences and lifestyle. This flexibility can lead to higher satisfaction and adherence in the long run, which is essential for maintaining weight loss.

Embracing this diet also means embracing a journey of discovery about nutrition and how it impacts your body. It encourages experimenting with different types of foods on different days, which can be an enjoyable process of discovering new meals and flavors that not only contribute to weight loss but also enhance your overall health.

Furthermore, this diet plan can be a powerful tool in managing blood sugar levels, an important aspect for many women over 50, particularly those dealing with insulin sensitivity or type 2 diabetes. Regularly alternating your carbohydrate intake can help improve insulin sensitivity and better regulate blood sugar levels, potentially reducing the risk of diabetes complications.

It's important to note, however, that while the Metabolic Confusion Diet offers numerous benefits, it's crucial to approach it with a well-informed perspective. Consulting with a healthcare provider or a dietitian before starting any new diet, especially one involving significant changes to carbohydrate intake, is essential. They can help tailor the diet even further to your individual health needs, ensuring that you receive all the necessary nutrients without compromising your health.

Lastly, remember that any successful diet is just one component of a healthy lifestyle. Combining the Metabolic Confusion Diet with regular physical activity, adequate hydration, and sufficient sleep will amplify your results, helping you not only lose weight but also gain vitality, improve your mood, and enhance your overall quality of life.

As you embark on this exciting new chapter, keep in mind that the journey to optimal health is personal and can require patience and perseverance. Each step you take with the Metabolic Confusion Diet is a step towards understanding your body better, mastering your metabolism, and reclaiming a vibrant, energetic life even after 50. Embrace the journey with enthusiasm and an open mind, and you'll discover that this can be a transformative and deeply rewarding process.

How This Book Will Transform Your Diet and Metabolism

Embarking on the Metabolic Confusion Diet, as outlined in this book, represents a significant shift not just in how you eat but in how your body processes what you eat. This transformation can rejuvenate your metabolism and set you on a path to sustainable weight loss, particularly impactful for endomorph women over 50, who often face unique metabolic challenges due to hormonal changes and a naturally slower metabolic rate.

This diet is designed to 'confuse' your metabolic processes, shaking up the routine to which your body has grown accustomed. The idea is straightforward yet scientifically profound: by regularly changing your intake of carbohydrates, your metabolism doesn't have time to adapt to any one pattern. This lack of adaptation keeps your metabolic rate on its toes, so to speak, potentially increasing its speed and efficiency over time.

One of the primary ways this diet impacts your body is through the process known as thermogenesis, the production of heat in the body generated from digesting food. Different foods ignite different levels of thermogenic activity, with carbohydrates and proteins causing the most significant increases. On days when your carbohydrate intake is higher, your body ramps up its energy expenditure to process these macronutrients, leading to higher caloric burn. Then, on low-carb days, your body, finding fewer carbohydrates to convert into glucose, turns to stored fat as its primary energy source. This shift not only aids in fat loss but also encourages your body to maintain this fat-burning mode longer.

Additionally, the diet enhances insulin sensitivity. As you grow older, your body's response to insulin can become less efficient, especially if your diet consists largely of high-glycemic foods that spike blood sugar levels. The carb cycling approach of the Metabolic Confusion Diet helps regulate blood sugar and improve insulin response, which is crucial for metabolism and overall health. Improved insulin sensitivity means your body can manage blood sugar more effectively, reducing the risk of diabetes and making it easier to maintain or lose weight.

Moreover, this approach can lead to better nutrient absorption. On high-carb days, you're encouraged to consume nutrient-dense carbohydrates—such as fruits, vegetables, and whole grains—that are rich in vitamins, minerals, and fiber. These nutrients support overall health, including metabolic function, while fiber improves digestion and satiety, reducing the likelihood of overeating. Then, on protein-focused days, you provide your body with essential amino acids necessary for muscle repair and growth. Muscle mass is pivotal in boosting metabolic rate, as muscle tissue burns more calories at rest than fat tissue.

This diet also promotes a more mindful approach to eating, which can transform your dietary habits over the long term. By paying closer attention to what and when you eat, you become more attuned to your body's hunger signals and satiety cues, which can help prevent overeating—a common issue as we age and our energy needs decrease.

Incorporating the principles of the Metabolic Confusion Diet also encourages a variety of foods, which prevents the nutritional deficiencies that can occur with more restrictive diets. This variety not only keeps your meals interesting but ensures a well-rounded intake of all necessary nutrients, fostering overall health and well-being. Moreover, the flexibility of this diet plan means that it can be adapted to suit individual dietary needs and preferences, making it a practical choice for long-term adherence.

The psychological benefits of this diet should not be underestimated. Dieting can often feel like a chore, a repetitive and joyless process. The Metabolic Confusion Diet, with its alternating focus and flexible approach, injects an element of surprise and variety into your meal planning, which can make the process more engaging and less daunting. This psychological uplift is crucial in maintaining motivation, particularly important when the dieting process extends over a longer period.

Furthermore, the structure of the Metabolic Confusion Diet—with its built-in variability—encourages a break from the potential monotony of traditional diets. This can alleviate the diet fatigue that many experience, which often leads to the abandonment of the diet altogether. By continuously altering your eating patterns, you're less likely to feel bored and more likely to stick with your plan long enough to see significant results.

This book aims to not only explain the science behind these processes but also to provide you with the practical tools to implement them. By following the detailed guidance and tailored recipes included, you'll be able to kickstart your metabolism, embrace a healthier lifestyle, and achieve weight loss that is not just rapid but also sustainable. The journey towards a transformed diet and revitalized metabolism begins with understanding and applying the principles laid out in this book, setting the stage for a healthier, more vibrant you.

1

METABOLIC MASTERY FOR MATURE WOMEN

Understanding the unique metabolic challenges that mature women face is essential for effective weight management and overall health. As women age, especially after 50, hormonal changes can significantly slow down the metabolic rate, making weight loss more challenging. The decrease in estrogen levels, in particular, affects how the body stores fat and manages hunger cues, often leading to increased abdominal fat and fluctuations in appetite. Moreover, muscle mass naturally decreases with age, which further slows metabolism because muscle burns more calories than fat, even at rest. Recognizing these changes, it's crucial for dietary approaches to adapt accordingly. A diet that not only focuses on weight loss but also enhances metabolic health can make a profound difference. By tailoring nutritional intake to the body's evolving needs, mature women can better manage their weight and improve their overall vitality. This is where understanding and embracing a diet that responds to these metabolic shifts not only becomes beneficial but essential.

Understanding Endomorph Basics at 50+

The endomorph body type is one of three commonly recognized somatotypes that describe the human physique and metabolic tendencies. Endomorphs are often characterized by a higher proportion of body fat, a rounder physique, and a significant challenge in losing weight. Understanding the specific challenges and changes associated with being an endomorph over the age of 50 is crucial for managing health and wellness effectively.

As people age, especially women over 50, their bodies undergo various hormonal and metabolic changes that can affect their physical health, weight, and overall well-being. For endomorphs, these changes can be particularly impactful. The most notable change is the shift in hormonal balance due to menopause. Estrogen levels drop significantly during and after menopause, which can lead to several metabolic slowdowns. Since estrogen helps regulate body weight and metabolism, its reduction can make it even harder for endomorphs to maintain or lose weight.

Furthermore, with age, there tends to be a natural decrease in muscle mass, a condition known as sarcopenia. Since muscle tissue burns more calories than fat tissue, even at rest, the loss of muscle mass can slow down the metabolic rate significantly. This reduction in basal metabolic rate means that without adjustments in diet or physical activity, weight gain is more likely. For endomorphs, who naturally have a slower metabolism, this muscle loss can exacerbate the challenge of preventing weight gain.

Another factor affecting endomorphs over 50 is insulin sensitivity, which tends to decrease with age. Lower insulin sensitivity can lead to higher blood sugar levels and can make the body store fat more readily, particularly around the abdomen. This change not only influences weight but also impacts overall metabolic health, increasing the risk of developing type 2 diabetes and other metabolic syndromes.

Moreover, as endomorphs age, their bodies' ability to recover from exercise and stress can diminish, making high-intensity workouts more challenging and less frequent. This reduction in physical activity can further decrease the metabolic rate, creating a cycle of weight gain that can be tough to break. It becomes essential for endomorphs to adapt their exercise routines to include more low-impact, resistance-based exercises that promote muscle maintenance and metabolic activation without excessive strain.

The diet also plays a critical role in managing the endomorph body type after 50. As metabolism slows, the caloric needs decrease. It becomes increasingly important to focus on the quality of the diet rather than just the calorie content. High-fiber, nutrient-dense foods that are lower in calories but high in satiety can help manage weight and support metabolic health. Managing carbohydrate intake is particularly crucial, as endomorphs tend to convert excess carbohydrates into fat more readily than other body types.

Additionally, managing stress and ensuring adequate sleep are vital components of weight management for endomorphs over 50. Stress can lead to increased cortisol levels, which promote fat storage, particularly in the abdominal area. Similarly, poor sleep can disrupt hormones that regulate appetite and metabolism, such as ghrelin and leptin. Therefore, adopting strategies to reduce stress and improve sleep quality can have a direct positive effect on weight management and metabolic health.

Being an endomorph over 50 requires a thoughtful approach to diet and lifestyle. It involves understanding the unique physiological changes that occur with age and how they affect metabolism and body composition. With strategic dietary choices, appropriate exercise, and lifestyle adjustments, endomorph women over 50 can manage their weight effectively and maintain a healthy metabolism. This understanding is not just about adapting to limitations but embracing the opportunity to optimize health and vitality in later life. It's about recognizing the challenges and transforming them into a structured plan that enhances quality of life and promotes longevity.

The Science of Aging and Metabolism

Ageing brings about a complex array of changes in the body, particularly affecting metabolism. Understanding these changes is crucial for managing health and wellness as we grow older. As individuals age, their metabolic rate generally declines, which can have significant implications for energy levels, weight management, and overall health.

The metabolic rate is essentially the rate at which the body converts food into energy to maintain vital functions. In youth, a higher metabolic rate supports growth and the high energy demands of developing bodies. However, as we age, several factors contribute to a decrease in this rate. One primary factor is the natural loss of muscle mass that occurs with age, known as sarcopenia. Muscle tissue is metabolically active, meaning it burns calories even at rest, much more so than fat tissue. As muscle mass decreases, fewer calories are burned, which can lead to weight gain if caloric intake is not adjusted accordingly.

Another significant aspect of ageing is the change in hormonal balance. Hormones play a crucial role in regulating metabolism. For instance, thyroid hormones are instrumental in setting basal metabolic rate. With age, the production of these hormones can decrease, leading to a slower metabolism. Similarly, the decrease in sex hormones like estrogen and testosterone also impacts body composition and metabolism. In women, the drop in estrogen during menopause often leads to increased fat accumulation around the abdomen, a shift from earlier fat storage in the hips and thighs. This type of fat is not only harder to lose but also contributes to a higher risk of cardiovascular disease and insulin resistance.

Insulin resistance itself becomes more common with age. The cells in the body become less responsive to insulin, a hormone that regulates blood sugar levels by facilitating the transfer of glucose into cells to be used for energy. When cells become insulin resistant, glucose levels in the blood remain high, and the body is prompted to release even more insulin. High insulin levels promote fat storage, particularly around the abdomen, and increase the risk of developing type 2 diabetes.

Furthermore, ageing affects the body's ability to use and store energy efficiently. Mitochondrial function, where energy production occurs at the cellular level, declines with age. This decline in mitochondrial efficiency leads to decreased energy levels and can accelerate the decline in metabolic health. Moreover, the body's thermogenic response to food—the heat produced during digestion that also consumes calories—diminishes with age. This means that older adults burn fewer calories when processing their meals compared to younger people.

Ageing also influences appetite and dietary patterns, which in turn affect metabolism. Changes in taste, digestive function, and appetite often accompany ageing, sometimes leading to reduced caloric intake, which might not adequately meet nutritional needs. On the other hand, some may find it difficult to adjust their eating habits to match their slowing metabolism, resulting in calorie excesses and weight gain.

To manage these age-related metabolic changes effectively, it's important to adopt a diet that accommodates the body's changing needs. This includes increasing the intake of high-fiber foods, which help manage blood sugar levels and improve satiety, and protein-rich foods to support muscle mass and counteract sarcopenia. Regular physical activity, particularly strength training, is crucial as it helps maintain muscle mass, supports metabolic rate, and improves insulin sensitivity.

Moreover, lifestyle factors such as sleep and stress management play significant roles. Poor sleep has been linked to imbalances in the hormones that control appetite, namely ghrelin and leptin, which can lead to increased hunger and weight gain. Chronic stress, meanwhile, elevates cortisol levels, which can lead to insulin resistance and fat accumulation around the midsection.

In essence, the science of ageing and metabolism underscores a shift towards slower metabolic processes and altered body composition. However, with strategic dietary adjustments, consistent physical activity, and effective management of lifestyle factors like stress and sleep, these changes can be managed. The goal in understanding these metabolic shifts is not merely to extend life but to enhance the quality of life in later years, ensuring that one remains active, healthy, and vibrant well into old age.

Tailoring the Metabolic Confusion Diet to Your Life Stage

Adapting the Metabolic Confusion Diet to the specific life stage of older adults involves understanding the unique health and lifestyle needs that come with ageing. This diet, which revolves around varying macronutrient intake to keep the metabolism active and guessing, can be particularly beneficial for individuals over 50 who often face metabolic slowdowns and increased health risks.

The primary appeal of the Metabolic Confusion Diet is its flexibility, which allows it to be customized according to individual needs, preferences, and health conditions prevalent among older adults. As metabolism naturally slows down with age, managing calorie intake becomes crucial. This diet facilitates this by alternating between high-carb and low-carb days, which can help manage and even boost the metabolic rate without the monotony of a constant caloric restriction, which is often unsustainable and unpalatable for many.

For older adults, particularly those who are less active due to physical constraints or those experiencing a natural decline in energy levels, high-carb days provide the necessary energy to remain active and engaged in daily activities. These days can be strategically planned on more active days when energy expenditure is higher. Conversely, low-carb days can be scheduled on less active days to aid in fat-burning and prevent the accumulation of unused calories.

Incorporating a higher protein intake on all days is also beneficial. Protein is crucial for preserving muscle mass, which tends to diminish with age. Sarcopenia, the age-related loss of muscle mass and strength, significantly contributes to a decline in metabolic rate and can increase the risk of falls and fractures. High-quality proteins, which include lean meats, fish, eggs, and plant-based sources like beans and lentils, should be a staple in the diet. Proteins not only help in muscle maintenance but also promote satiety and have a higher thermogenic effect than fats or carbohydrates, meaning the body uses more energy to digest protein.

Hydration is another key aspect that must be tailored to the diet of older adults. With ageing, the body's ability to conserve water is reduced, and the sense of thirst may not be as acute. Ensuring adequate fluid intake is essential for maintaining kidney function and overall cellular health. In the Metabolic Confusion Diet, where the intake of proteins and fibers is high, increasing water intake is important to help manage digestion and metabolic processes.

The diet also needs to address the common micronutrient deficiencies that can occur in older adults, such as deficiencies in vitamin D, calcium, and B vitamins. Vitamin D and calcium are vital for maintaining bone health, while B vitamins are essential for energy production and maintaining proper brain function. Including a variety of fruits, vegetables, fortified foods, and possibly supplements, as advised by a healthcare provider, can help manage these needs.

Furthermore, the dietary approach must consider the ease of meal preparation and the enjoyment of food. Meals that are simple to prepare, appealing, and flavorful can encourage regular eating and ensure that nutritional needs are met. This is particularly important as taste and smell senses may diminish with age, and appetite can decrease. Experimenting with herbs and spices, varying meal textures, and incorporating favorite foods can help enhance meal enjoyment.

Tailoring the diet also involves aligning it with any medical guidance provided for existing health conditions like hypertension, diabetes, or heart disease. For instance, if an individual has insulin resistance or type 2 diabetes, managing carbohydrate quality and quantity on high-carb days becomes crucial. Opting for complex carbohydrates with a low glycemic index, which causes a slower rise in blood glucose levels, is a strategic choice.

Lastly, adapting the Metabolic Confusion Diet for older adults means integrating it into a holistic lifestyle approach that includes physical activity, social interactions, and adequate rest. Encouraging regular, moderate exercise can enhance the effectiveness of the diet by boosting metabolism and improving mood and cognitive function. Social meals can also provide motivation for preparing balanced, nutritious foods, while proper rest and recovery are crucial for metabolic health.

In essence, tailoring the Metabolic Confusion Diet to fit the lifestyle and health needs of older adults is about more than just weight management. It's about enhancing the quality of life, maintaining independence, and promoting longevity through thoughtful, personalized dietary adjustments. This adaptive approach allows each individual to address their specific health challenges and preferences, making the diet a sustainable part of a healthy ageing strategy.

2

THE PRINCIPLES OF METABOLIC CONFUSION

The principles of Metabolic Confusion are designed to stimulate and revitalize your metabolism by introducing variety into your diet. This approach hinges on alternating between different levels of macronutrient intake, primarily carbohydrates, which prevents your body from settling into a predictable routine. Typically, on a traditional diet, the body adapts to the dietary patterns, which can lead to a plateau in weight loss and metabolic rate. However, by varying your carbohydrate and calorie intake regularly, the Metabolic Confusion diet keeps your metabolic processes actively adjusting and working, which can lead to improved fat-burning and energy levels. This method offers a dynamic way of eating that can adapt to your lifestyle and preferences, making it more sustainable and enjoyable than diets with strict, unchanging rules.

It's particularly effective because it aligns with the body's natural need for balance and change, supporting overall health while promoting weight loss. By implementing this strategy, you engage in a proactive form of nutrition that keeps your body guessing and metabolism firing, which can be especially beneficial as you age and your metabolic rate naturally begins to slow down.

What Is Metabolic Confusion?

Metabolic confusion is a dietary strategy designed to prevent the body from adapting to a specific caloric or macronutrient intake pattern. Traditional diets often fail because the body adjusts to the reduced caloric intake, leading to a plateau in weight loss. Metabolic confusion counters this by regularly changing dietary intake, keeping the metabolism active and guessing. This method is believed to enhance fat loss while maintaining muscle mass, improve metabolic flexibility, and prevent weight loss plateaus.

At its core, metabolic confusion is about variability. It involves alternating between high-calorie and low-calorie days or high-carb and low-carb days, depending on the specific approach. This fluctuation is thought to stimulate the metabolism, potentially increasing the number of calories burned and preventing the body from entering a state of metabolic adaptation, where it becomes highly efficient at conserving energy.

The rationale behind metabolic confusion is rooted in our evolutionary biology. Historically, human beings did not have access to a consistent food supply, so our bodies evolved to be adaptable to varying food intakes. By mimicking this irregular food availability, metabolic confusion aims to optimize the metabolic rate, which is the rate at which the body burns calories.

This dietary approach has several intended metabolic impacts. First, it aims to boost the basal metabolic rate (BMR), which is the number of calories required to keep your body functioning at rest. The theory is that by constantly changing your energy intake, your metabolism doesn't slow down as it typically would on a traditional calorie-restricted diet. Instead, on high-calorie days, the body ramps up its energy production to process the increased intake, and on low-calorie days, it turns to stored fat for energy, which can lead to effective fat burning.

Second, metabolic confusion can lead to improved insulin sensitivity. On days when carbohydrate intake is higher, the body's insulin response is stimulated, which can help manage blood sugar levels. On low-carb days, the reduced demand for insulin gives the body a break from insulin production, potentially helping to reset insulin sensitivity. This can be particularly beneficial for individuals with insulin resistance or type 2 diabetes.

Furthermore, the diet promotes a balanced intake of nutrients by encouraging a diverse range of foods on different days. This variability not only helps cover a broad spectrum of vitamins and minerals but also prevents the dietary boredom that often accompanies more restrictive regimens. By incorporating a wide variety of foods, the diet ensures that no nutrient deficiencies occur while keeping the diet interesting and more sustainable.

Another significant impact of metabolic confusion is on appetite control. Fluctuating calorie intake can help regulate the hormones that control hunger and satiety, such as ghrelin and leptin. On high-calorie days, the body experiences satiety and an abundance of energy, which can help reduce cravings and control overeating on subsequent low-calorie days. This hormonal regulation can aid in long-term weight management and reduce the likelihood of binge eating.

Moreover, metabolic confusion can enhance mental resilience and flexibility toward eating. By not restricting any particular food group completely, it encourages a healthier relationship with food. Individuals learn to adjust their eating patterns flexibly, which can alleviate the stress and psychological strain often associated with strict dietary restrictions.

Finally, this approach can lead to a more active lifestyle. With varying levels of carbohydrate and calorie intake, individuals may find they have more energy on certain days, which can encourage more physical activity. This increase in activity not only aids in additional calorie burn but also contributes to overall health and well-being.

Metabolic confusion is more than just a diet; it's a comprehensive approach to eating that considers the body's natural rhythms and evolutionary history. By integrating this strategy into one's lifestyle, it is possible to enhance metabolic health, prevent dieting plateaus, and maintain a balanced and enjoyable eating plan. This method's flexibility and focus on long-term sustainability make it a compelling choice for those looking to manage their weight and improve their metabolic health effectively.

The Role of Carb Cycling in Fat Loss

Carb cycling is a strategic approach to dieting that involves varying carbohydrate intake on a daily, weekly, or monthly basis. It is designed to optimize fat loss and improve physical performance while also aiming to circumvent the metabolic slowdown associated with more traditional, static dieting methods. This approach can be particularly effective for fat loss as it aligns with the body's natural energy needs and hormonal responses.

The essence of carb cycling lies in its ability to manipulate the body's metabolism through intentional shifts in carbohydrate consumption. On days when more intense physical activity occurs, carb intake is increased to provide sufficient energy and support muscle recovery. Conversely, on rest or light activity days, carb intake is reduced. This variation helps to maximize the body's fat-burning capabilities while maintaining muscle mass, which is often a challenge with constant calorie-restricted diets.

One of the key mechanisms through which carb cycling aids in weight management is its impact on insulin levels. Insulin is a hormone that regulates blood glucose levels by facilitating the uptake of glucose into cells. High carb intake leads to increased blood sugar levels, which elevate insulin production. By strategically lowering carb intake at times, the body's sensitivity to insulin can be improved, preventing high spikes in insulin, which are linked to fat storage.

Further, by cycling carbohydrate intake, the body is often forced to tap into its fat stores for energy on low-carb days. This is because glycogen, the stored form of glucose in muscles and the liver, becomes depleted during lower-carb periods. The body then turns to fat as an alternative energy source, leading to increased fat oxidation or the breakdown of fat cells for energy, which directly contributes to fat loss.

Moreover, the psychological benefits of carb cycling should not be underestimated. Dietary adherence can often be the downfall of many strict nutritional regimes. Carb cycling allows for greater flexibility, making it easier to stick with the diet long-term. It accommodates social meals and high-carb cravings, which might otherwise derail a more restrictive diet. By planning higher carb days during social events or during intense workouts, individuals can enjoy a varied diet that fits their lifestyle while still achieving their weight loss goals.

Another advantage of carb cycling is its potential to prevent the metabolic plateau commonly experienced in continuous calorie-restricted diets. When calorie intake is consistently low, the body can adapt by lowering its metabolic rate as a survival mechanism. This adaptive thermogenesis can make further weight loss challenging. However, the periodic refeeding provided by high-carb days in carb cycling can help maintain metabolic rate by reassuring the body that starvation is not imminent.

In addition to managing weight, carb cycling can have profound impacts on overall health. For instance, it can help manage or prevent diseases associated with poor insulin management, such as type 2 diabetes. By improving insulin sensitivity and blood sugar control, carb cycling not only aids in fat loss but also enhances the body's ability to manage glucose levels, reducing risk factors associated with insulin resistance and diabetes.

Furthermore, the inclusion of high-carb days ensures that the body receives enough nutrients to support thyroid function, which is crucial for regulating metabolism. Thyroid hormones are sensitive to extreme dieting conditions, and insufficient carbohydrate consumption can lead to decreased thyroid hormone production, subsequently slowing metabolism. Carb cycling can help support thyroid health by providing periodic boosts in carb intake, which can stimulate thyroid activity and hence keep metabolic rates favorable for weight loss.

Carb cycling also supports gut health by varying the types of foods consumed, which can encourage a diverse microbiome. This diversity is crucial for overall health, as a healthy gut can improve everything from immune function to mental health. The variability in fiber intake from different carbohydrates can foster a robust gut microbiome, further supporting digestion and nutrient absorption.

Overall, carb cycling offers a nuanced approach to diet that goes beyond simple calorie restriction. It considers the body's hormonal environment, energy needs, psychological factors, and metabolic health, providing a dynamic framework that can be adapted to fit individual preferences and lifestyles. This adaptability not only helps in effective fat loss but also supports sustainable health improvements, making carb cycling a viable and strategic option for those looking to manage their weight and enhance their overall health.

Variability and Your Metabolic Rate

Variability in your metabolic rate is a concept at the heart of many modern dietary strategies, including the increasingly popular metabolic confusion approach. By introducing variability into your diet, you can effectively influence how your body processes energy and nutrients, which can have profound benefits on overall metabolic health.

A variable metabolic rate means that your body's metabolism does not remain constant but fluctuates in response to various factors such as diet, physical activity, and even the time of day. This variability can be a significant advantage for weight management and health, as it encourages the body to adapt to different conditions, enhancing its ability to regulate weight and respond to dietary changes.

One of the primary benefits of promoting a variable metabolic rate is improved fat burning. Traditional diets often lead to a metabolic slowdown because the body adapts to a consistently lower calorie intake by reducing its basal metabolic rate (BMR) — the amount of energy expended while at rest. This adaptation can make continued weight loss difficult. However, by varying calorie and carbohydrate intake, you prevent the body from settling into this energy-conserving mode. On days with higher calorie intake, the body boosts its energy expenditure, and on lower-calorie days, it turns to stored fat for energy, enhancing overall fat loss.

This approach also benefits insulin sensitivity, a critical aspect of metabolic health. Constant high carbohydrate or calorie intake can lead to increased blood glucose levels and consequently higher insulin production, which over time can lead to insulin resistance — a condition where the body's cells do not respond properly to insulin, leading to higher blood sugar levels. By varying carbohydrate intake, not only are these spikes in blood sugar controlled, but the body's response to insulin can improve, reducing the risk of diabetes and other metabolic disorders.

Moreover, a variable metabolic rate can lead to better long-term adherence to a diet. Fixed dietary regimens can be challenging to maintain due to their restrictive nature and the psychological burden they often carry. In contrast, a diet that includes variability is less likely to become monotonous and allows for more flexibility, which can lead to higher satisfaction and easier integration into different lifestyles and preferences.

Further, varying your metabolic rate can enhance your body's resilience. Just as muscles grow stronger when exposed to varying physical challenges, metabolic pathways can become more efficient when they are regularly 'tested' by different nutritional environments.

This metabolic flexibility can help the body better cope with stressors such as fasting, overeating, and physical stress, improving overall health and reducing the likelihood of chronic diseases.

Another important aspect is the prevention of metabolic adaptation, where the body becomes very efficient at using a small amount of energy for its daily needs. This efficiency, while seemingly beneficial, can be a disadvantage for those trying to lose weight because it can stall progress. By keeping the metabolism guessing, you encourage it to maintain a higher level of activity even on days of lower calorie intake, which can prevent plateaus in weight loss.

Furthermore, introducing variability can help maintain and even build muscle mass. Muscle is metabolically active tissue, meaning it burns calories even when at rest. Diets that include days of higher protein and calorie intake can support muscle synthesis and maintenance, which is especially important as we age and naturally begin to lose muscle mass, a condition known as sarcopenia.

In addition, a variable metabolic rate can improve overall energy levels. Alternating between higher and lower calorie days can prevent the common energy dips associated with constant calorie-restricted diets. On high-calorie days, the body receives more fuel, potentially increasing energy levels, while on low-calorie days, the enhanced fat burning can also lead to a more, steady supply of energy, avoiding the crashes often seen in strict low-calorie or low-carb diets.

Finally, the psychological benefits of this approach should not be underestimated. Dietary flexibility can reduce feelings of deprivation and diet-related stress, making it easier to adhere to healthy eating patterns in the long term. This psychological ease is crucial for sustainable weight management and overall well-being.

Introducing variability into your metabolic rate through a flexible dietary approach can offer numerous benefits. It enhances the body's ability to burn fat, improves insulin sensitivity, supports muscle maintenance, increases dietary adherence, and boosts overall energy levels. This approach not only aids in effective weight management but also contributes to a healthier, more resilient metabolic system.

4

100 RECIPES

Breakfast

Spinach and Feta Omelet

Ingredients:

- 2 large eggs
- 1 cup fresh spinach, chopped
- 1/4 cup feta cheese, crumbled
- 1 tablespoon olive oil
- Salt and pepper to taste

Instructions:

1. In a bowl, whisk the eggs with salt and pepper.
2. Heat olive oil in a skillet over medium heat. Add the chopped spinach and sauté until wilted.
3. Pour the eggs over the spinach and sprinkle crumbled feta on top.
4. Cook until the eggs are set and fold the omelet in half. Serve warm.

Nutritional Values (per serving):

- Protein: Helps in muscle repair and growth.
- Iron: Essential for blood cell production found in spinach.
- Calcium: Supports bone health from feta cheese.

Almond Flour Pancakes with Blueberry Syrup

Ingredients:

- 1 cup almond flour
- 2 eggs
- 1/2 cup milk
- 1 teaspoon baking powder
- 1 cup blueberries
- 1/4 cup honey

Instructions:

1. In a bowl, combine almond flour and baking powder.
2. Mix in eggs and milk to form a batter.

3. Heat a non-stick pan and pour batter to form pancakes, flipping once until golden on both sides.

4. For the syrup, heat blueberries and honey in a saucepan until berries burst. Pour over pancakes.

Nutritional Values (per serving):

- Fiber: Promotes digestive health from almond flour.

- Antioxidants: Prevent cellular damage from blueberries.

- Protein: Essential for body repair from eggs.

Greek Yogurt Parfait with Nuts and Berries

Ingredients:

- 1 cup Greek yogurt

- 1/2 cup mixed berries (strawberries, blueberries, raspberries)

- 1/4 cup mixed nuts (almonds, walnuts, pecans), chopped

- 1 tablespoon honey

Instructions:

1. In a glass, layer Greek yogurt, mixed berries, and chopped nuts.

2. Repeat the layers until all ingredients are used.

3. Drizzle honey on top before serving.

Nutritional Values (per serving):

- Probiotics: Enhance gut health from Greek yogurt.

- Omega-3 fatty acids: Improve heart health from nuts.

- Vitamins: Boost immune system from berries.

Smoked Salmon and Avocado Toast on Whole Grain Bread

Ingredients:

- 2 slices whole grain bread

- 1 avocado, sliced

- 100g smoked salmon

- 1 tablespoon lemon juice

- Salt and pepper to taste

Instructions:

1. Toast the bread slices until golden and crispy.

2. Mash the avocado with lemon juice, salt, and pepper, and spread over the toasted bread.

3. Top with smoked salmon and serve immediately.

Nutritional Values (per serving):

- Omega-3 fatty acids: Reduce inflammation from salmon.

- Fiber: Aids digestion from whole grain bread.

- Healthy fats: Support cardiovascular health from avocado.

Cottage Cheese and Pineapple Bowl

Ingredients:

- 1 cup cottage cheese

- 1/2 cup chopped pineapple

- 1 tablespoon chia seeds

- 1 teaspoon honey (optional)

Instructions:

1. In a bowl, combine cottage cheese and chopped pineapple.

2. Sprinkle chia seeds over the top and drizzle with honey if desired.

3. Serve chilled as a refreshing snack or breakfast.

Nutritional Values (per serving):

- Protein: Builds and repairs tissues from cottage cheese.

- Vitamin C: Strengthens immune system from pineapple.

- Omega-3 fatty acids: Improve heart health from chia seeds.

Turkey Sausage and Sweet Potato Hash

Ingredients:

- 2 turkey sausages, sliced

- 1 large sweet potato, peeled and diced

- 1/2 red bell pepper, chopped

- 1/2 green bell pepper, chopped

- 1 small onion, diced

- 2 tablespoons olive oil

- Salt and pepper to taste

Instructions:

1. Heat olive oil in a large skillet over medium heat. Add the diced sweet potato and cook until slightly softened.

2. Add the onion and bell peppers to the skillet, cooking until the vegetables are tender.

3. Add the turkey sausage slices and cook until browned and heated through.

4. Season with salt and pepper, then serve hot.

Nutritional Values (per serving):

- Protein: Essential for muscle repair from turkey sausage.

- Beta-carotene: Supports vision health from sweet potatoes.

- Fiber: Promotes digestive health from vegetables.

Protein-Packed Smoothie Bowl with Chia Seeds

Ingredients:

- 1 banana, frozen

- 1/2 cup Greek yogurt

- 1/2 cup almond milk

- 1 scoop protein powder

- 1 tablespoon chia seeds

- 1/4 cup granola

- 1/4 cup mixed berries

Instructions:

1. Blend the frozen banana, Greek yogurt, almond milk, and protein powder until smooth.

2. Pour the smoothie into a bowl and top with chia seeds, granola, and mixed berries.

3. Enjoy immediately for a refreshing and nutritious breakfast.

Nutritional Values (per serving):

- Protein: Supports muscle recovery from protein powder and Greek yogurt.

- Omega-3 fatty acids: Promote heart health from chia seeds.

- Antioxidants: Protect against free radicals from mixed berries.

Egg White Scramble with Asparagus and Tomatoes

Ingredients:

- 4 egg whites

- 1/2 cup asparagus, chopped

- 1/2 cup cherry tomatoes, halved

- 1 tablespoon olive oil

- Salt and pepper to taste

Instructions:

1. Heat olive oil in a skillet over medium heat. Add the asparagus and cook until tender.

2. Add the cherry tomatoes and cook for an additional 2 minutes.

3. Pour in the egg whites and scramble until cooked through.

4. Season with salt and pepper, then serve hot.

Nutritional Values (per serving):

- Protein: Low in fat, high in protein from egg whites.

- Vitamins: Enhance immune function from asparagus.

- Lycopene: Supports heart health from tomatoes.

Low-Carb Almond Butter Waffles

Ingredients:

- 1 cup almond flour

- 2 eggs

- 1/4 cup almond butter

- 1/4 cup almond milk

- 1 teaspoon baking powder

- 1 teaspoon vanilla extract

Instructions:

1. In a bowl, whisk together almond flour, baking powder, eggs, almond butter, almond milk, and vanilla extract until smooth.

2. Preheat a waffle iron and lightly grease with oil.

3. Pour the batter into the waffle iron and cook until golden brown.

4. Serve warm with your favorite toppings.

Nutritional Values (per serving):

- Protein: Aids muscle building from eggs and almond butter.

- Healthy fats: Promote satiety from almond flour and almond butter.

- Low-carb: Suitable for low-carb diets.

Quinoa Porridge with Cinnamon and Apple

Ingredients:

- 1/2 cup quinoa
- 1 cup almond milk
- 1 apple, diced
- 1 teaspoon cinnamon
- 1 tablespoon maple syrup
- 1/4 cup chopped walnuts

Instructions:

1. Rinse quinoa under cold water and drain.
2. In a saucepan, combine quinoa and almond milk. Bring to a boil, then reduce heat and simmer until quinoa is tender.
3. Stir in the diced apple, cinnamon, and maple syrup.
4. Serve topped with chopped walnuts.

Nutritional Values (per serving):

- Protein: Complete protein source from quinoa.
- Fiber: Supports digestion from apple and quinoa.
- Antioxidants: Enhance overall health from cinnamon.

Breakfast Tacos with Scrambled Eggs and Spinach

Ingredients:

- 4 small corn tortillas
- 4 eggs
- 1 cup spinach, chopped
- 1/2 cup shredded cheese
- 1 tablespoon olive oil
- Salt and pepper to taste

Instructions:

1. Heat olive oil in a skillet over medium heat. Add the spinach and cook until wilted.
2. Whisk the eggs and pour into the skillet, scrambling until cooked through.
3. Warm the tortillas in a separate pan.
4. Fill each tortilla with scrambled eggs, spinach, and shredded cheese.
5. Serve immediately.

Nutritional Values (per serving):

- Protein: Supports muscle growth from eggs.
- Fiber: Aids digestion from spinach and tortillas.
- Calcium: Strengthens bones from cheese.

Chia Pudding with Coconut Milk and Mango

Ingredients:

- 1/2 cup chia seeds
- 2 cups coconut milk
- 1 tablespoon honey
- 1 cup mango, diced

Instructions:

1. In a bowl, combine chia seeds, coconut milk, and honey. Stir well.

2. Refrigerate for at least 4 hours or overnight, stirring occasionally.

3. Top with diced mango before serving.

Nutritional Values (per serving):

- Omega-3 fatty acids: Promote heart health from chia seeds.

- Healthy fats: Support brain function from coconut milk.

- Vitamins: Boost immune system from mango.

Turkey Bacon and Avocado Wrap

Ingredients:

- 2 whole grain tortillas

- 4 slices turkey bacon

- 1 avocado, sliced

- 1/2 cup lettuce, shredded

- 1 tomato, sliced

- 1 tablespoon mayonnaise

Instructions:

1. Cook turkey bacon in a skillet until crispy.

2. Spread mayonnaise on each tortilla.

3. Layer with turkey bacon, avocado, lettuce, and tomato.

4. Roll up the tortillas and serve.

Nutritional Values (per serving):

- Protein: Supports muscle repair from turkey bacon.

- Healthy fats: Promote heart health from avocado.

- Fiber: Supports digestion from whole grain tortillas and vegetables.

Keto Muffins with Spinach and Cheese

Ingredients:

- 1 cup almond flour

- 4 eggs

- 1/2 cup shredded cheese

- 1 cup spinach, chopped

- 1 teaspoon baking powder

- Salt and pepper to taste

Instructions:

1. Preheat oven to 350°F (175°C) and line a muffin tin with paper liners.

2. In a bowl, mix almond flour, baking powder, eggs, cheese, spinach, salt, and pepper until well combined.

3. Pour the mixture into the muffin tin, filling each cup about 3/4 full.

4. Bake for 20-25 minutes or until golden brown.

5. Let cool slightly before serving.

Nutritional Values (per serving):

- Protein: Aids muscle building from eggs and cheese.

- Healthy fats: Provide satiety from almond flour.

- Low-carb: Suitable for ketogenic diets.

Oatmeal with Pumpkin Seeds and Pears

Ingredients:

- 1 cup rolled oats
- 2 cups water or milk
- 1 pear, diced
- 1/4 cup pumpkin seeds
- 1 tablespoon honey
- 1 teaspoon cinnamon

Instructions:

1. In a saucepan, bring water or milk to a boil. Add oats and reduce heat to simmer.
2. Cook until oats are tender, stirring occasionally.
3. Stir in diced pear, pumpkin seeds, honey, and cinnamon.
4. Serve warm.

Nutritional Values (per serving):

- Fiber: Promotes digestion from oats and pear.
- Healthy fats: Support heart health from pumpkin seeds.
- Antioxidants: Improve overall health from cinnamon.

Ricotta and Berry Crepes

Ingredients:

- 1 cup flour
- 2 eggs
- 1 cup milk
- 1/2 cup ricotta cheese
- 1 cup mixed berries
- 1 tablespoon honey
- 1 teaspoon vanilla extract

Instructions:

1. In a bowl, whisk flour, eggs, milk, and vanilla extract until smooth.
2. Heat a non-stick skillet and pour a small amount of batter, spreading it thinly.
3. Cook until edges lift, then flip and cook the other side.
4. Fill crepes with ricotta cheese and berries, drizzle with honey.
5. Serve warm.

Nutritional Values (per serving):

- Protein: Supports muscle repair from eggs and ricotta.
- Antioxidants: Protect against free radicals from berries.
- Vitamins: Boost immune system from mixed berries.

Egg Muffins with Broccoli and Cheese

Ingredients:

- 6 eggs
- 1 cup broccoli, chopped
- 1/2 cup shredded cheese
- 1/4 cup milk
- Salt and pepper to taste

Instructions:

1. Preheat oven to 350°F (175°C) and grease a muffin tin.

2. In a bowl, whisk eggs and milk together.

3. Stir in chopped broccoli, shredded cheese, salt, and pepper.

4. Pour mixture into the muffin tin, filling each cup about 3/4 full.

5. Bake for 20-25 minutes or until eggs are set.

6. Let cool slightly before serving.

Nutritional Values (per serving):

- Protein: Essential for muscle repair from eggs and cheese.

- Fiber: Promotes digestive health from broccoli.

- Calcium: Supports bone health from cheese.

Sweet Pepper and Goat Cheese Frittata

Ingredients:

- 6 eggs

- 1/2 cup goat cheese, crumbled

- 1 cup sweet peppers, chopped

- 1/2 cup milk

- 1 tablespoon olive oil

- Salt and pepper to taste

Instructions:

1. Preheat oven to 375°F (190°C).

2. In a bowl, whisk eggs and milk together.

3. Heat olive oil in a skillet over medium heat. Add sweet peppers and cook until tender.

4. Pour egg mixture into the skillet, add goat cheese, and season with salt and pepper.

5. Transfer skillet to the oven and bake for 15-20 minutes or until eggs are set.

6. Let cool slightly before slicing and serving.

Nutritional Values (per serving):

- Protein: Aids muscle repair from eggs and goat cheese.

- Vitamins: Boost immune function from sweet peppers.

- Healthy fats: Support overall health from olive oil.

Banana Nut Protein Shake

Ingredients:

- 1 banana

- 1 cup almond milk

- 1 scoop protein powder

- 1 tablespoon almond butter

- 1 teaspoon honey

- 1/2 teaspoon cinnamon

Instructions:

1. Combine all ingredients in a blender and blend until smooth.

2. Serve immediately.

Nutritional Values (per serving):

- Protein: Supports muscle growth from protein powder.

- Potassium: Regulates fluid balance from banana.

- Healthy fats: Provide satiety from almond butter.

Savory Miso Oatmeal with Poached Egg

Ingredients:

- 1 cup rolled oats

- 2 cups water or broth

- 1 tablespoon miso paste

- 1 poached egg

- 1 green onion, chopped

- 1 tablespoon sesame seeds

Instructions:

1. In a saucepan, bring water or broth to a boil. Add oats and reduce heat to simmer.

2. Stir in miso paste until well combined.

3. Cook until oats are tender, then transfer to a bowl.

4. Top with a poached egg, chopped green onion, and sesame seeds.

5. Serve warm.

Nutritional Values (per serving):

- Protein: Essential for muscle repair from poached egg.

- Fiber: Promotes digestion from oats.

- Probiotics: Enhance gut health from miso paste.

Tofu and Vegetable Stir-fry

Ingredients:

- 1 block firm tofu, cubed

- 1 cup broccoli florets

- 1 bell pepper, sliced

- 1 carrot, julienned

- 1/2 cup snow peas

- 2 tablespoons soy sauce

- 1 tablespoon sesame oil

- 1 garlic clove, minced

- 1 tablespoon ginger, grated

- 2 tablespoons vegetable oil

Instructions:

1. Heat vegetable oil in a large skillet over medium-high heat. Add the cubed tofu and cook until golden brown on all sides.

2. Remove tofu from the skillet and set aside. In the same skillet, add sesame oil and sauté garlic and ginger until fragrant.

3. Add broccoli, bell pepper, carrot, and snow peas. Stir-fry until vegetables are tender-crisp.

4. Return the tofu to the skillet and add soy sauce. Toss to combine and heat through.

5. Serve hot, garnished with sesame seeds if desired.

Nutritional Values (per serving):

- Protein: Supports muscle repair from tofu.

- Vitamins: Enhance immune function from mixed vegetables.

- Antioxidants: Protect against free radicals from ginger.

Overnight Oats with Flaxseeds and Mixed Berries

Ingredients:

- 1 cup rolled oats

- 1 cup almond milk

- 2 tablespoons flaxseeds

- 1/2 cup mixed berries (strawberries, blueberries, raspberries)

- 1 tablespoon honey

- 1 teaspoon vanilla extract

Instructions:

1. In a jar or bowl, combine rolled oats, almond milk, flaxseeds, honey, and vanilla extract. Stir well.

2. Cover and refrigerate overnight.

3. In the morning, stir the oats and top with mixed berries before serving.

Nutritional Values (per serving):

- Fiber: Promotes digestion from oats and flaxseeds.

- Omega-3 fatty acids: Support heart health from flaxseeds.

- Antioxidants: Enhance overall health from berries.

Cottage Cheese with Sliced Peaches and Honey

Ingredients:

- 1 cup cottage cheese

- 1 large peach, sliced

- 1 tablespoon honey

- 1/4 teaspoon cinnamon

Instructions:

1. In a bowl, spoon the cottage cheese.

2. Arrange sliced peaches on top.

3. Drizzle with honey and sprinkle with cinnamon.

4. Serve chilled.

Nutritional Values (per serving):

- Protein: Builds and repairs tissues from cottage cheese.

- Vitamins: Boost immune function from peaches.

- Antioxidants: Protect cells from damage from cinnamon.

Multi-Grain Porridge with Mixed Nuts

Ingredients:

- 1/2 cup rolled oats

- 1/4 cup quinoa

- 1/4 cup millet

- 2 cups water or milk

- 1/4 cup mixed nuts (almonds, walnuts, pecans), chopped

- 1 tablespoon honey

- 1 teaspoon cinnamon

Instructions:

1. In a saucepan, combine rolled oats, quinoa, millet, and water or milk. Bring to a boil, then reduce heat and simmer until grains are tender.

2. Stir in honey and cinnamon.

3. Top with mixed nuts before serving.

Nutritional Values (per serving):

- Protein: Supports muscle repair from mixed grains and nuts.

- Fiber: Aids digestion from oats and quinoa.

- Healthy fats: Promote satiety from mixed nuts.

Avocado and Egg Salad on Rye Bread

Ingredients:

- 2 slices rye bread

- 1 avocado, mashed

- 2 hard-boiled eggs, chopped

- 1 tablespoon mayonnaise

- 1 teaspoon lemon juice

- Salt and pepper to taste

- Fresh herbs (optional)

Instructions:

1. In a bowl, combine chopped eggs, mayonnaise, lemon juice, salt, and pepper. Mix well.

2. Spread mashed avocado on rye bread slices.

3. Top with the egg salad mixture.

4. Garnish with fresh herbs if desired and serve.

Nutritional Values (per serving):

- Protein: Supports muscle repair from eggs.

- Healthy fats: Promote heart health from avocado.

- Fiber: Supports digestion from rye bread.

SCAN THE QR CODE AND IMMEDIATELY ACCESS YOUR 3 SPECIAL BONUSES IN DIGITAL FORMAT!

🔥 **Bonus 1: Dining Out Without Derailing Your Diet**

🔥 **Bonus 2: Recognizing Your Body Type**

🔥 **Bonus 3: Weekly Grocery Planner**

LUNCH

Grilled Chicken Caesar Salad

Ingredients:

- 2 boneless, skinless chicken breasts
- 1 romaine lettuce head, chopped
- 1/4 cup grated Parmesan cheese
- 1/2 cup Caesar dressing
- 1/2 cup croutons
- 1 tablespoon olive oil
- Salt and pepper to taste

Instructions:

1. Season chicken breasts with salt and pepper. Grill over medium heat until cooked through, about 6-7 minutes per side.

2. Let chicken rest for 5 minutes, then slice into strips.

3. In a large bowl, toss chopped romaine lettuce with Caesar dressing until well coated.

4. Top with grilled chicken slices, Parmesan cheese, and croutons.

5. Serve immediately.

Nutritional Values (per serving):

- Protein: Supports muscle repair from chicken.
- Vitamins: Enhance immune function from romaine lettuce.
- Healthy fats: Promote heart health from olive oil and Parmesan cheese.

Baked Falafel with Tzatziki Sauce

Ingredients:

- 1 can chickpeas, drained and rinsed
- 1 small onion, chopped
- 2 cloves garlic, minced
- 1/4 cup fresh parsley, chopped
- 2 tablespoons flour
- 1 teaspoon cumin
- 1 teaspoon coriander
- Salt and pepper to taste
- 2 tablespoons olive oil

Tzatziki Sauce:

- 1 cup Greek yogurt
- 1 cucumber, grated
- 1 tablespoon lemon juice
- 1 clove garlic, minced
- Salt and pepper to taste

Instructions:

1. Preheat oven to 375°F (190°C). In a food processor, combine chickpeas, onion, garlic, parsley, flour, cumin, coriander, salt, and pepper. Pulse until mixture is coarse but holds together.

2. Form into small patties and place on a baking sheet lined with parchment paper. Brush with olive oil.

3. Bake for 25-30 minutes, flipping halfway, until golden brown.

4. For the tzatziki sauce, combine Greek yogurt, grated cucumber, lemon juice, garlic, salt, and pepper in a bowl. Mix well.

5. Serve falafel warm with tzatziki sauce.

Nutritional Values (per serving):

- Protein: Supports muscle repair from chickpeas and Greek yogurt.

- Fiber: Promotes digestion from chickpeas.

- Probiotics: Enhance gut health from Greek yogurt.

Quinoa and Black Bean Salad

Ingredients:

- 1 cup quinoa

- 1 can black beans, drained and rinsed

- 1 cup corn kernels

- 1 red bell pepper, chopped

- 1/4 cup red onion, finely chopped

- 1/4 cup cilantro, chopped

- 1/4 cup lime juice

- 2 tablespoons olive oil

- Salt and pepper to taste

Instructions:

1. Cook quinoa according to package instructions and let cool.

2. In a large bowl, combine cooked quinoa, black beans, corn, red bell pepper, red onion, and cilantro.

3. In a small bowl, whisk together lime juice, olive oil, salt, and pepper. Pour over salad and toss to coat.

4. Serve chilled.

Nutritional Values (per serving):

- Protein: Supports muscle repair from quinoa and black beans.

- Fiber: Promotes digestion from quinoa and vegetables.

- Antioxidants: Protect against free radicals from red bell pepper and cilantro.

Turkey and Spinach Stuffed Bell Peppers

Ingredients:

- 4 bell peppers, tops cut off and seeds removed

- 1 pound ground turkey

- 1 cup cooked quinoa

- 1 cup spinach, chopped

- 1 small onion, chopped

- 1 can diced tomatoes

- 1 tablespoon olive oil

- 1 teaspoon garlic powder

- 1 teaspoon onion powder

- Salt and pepper to taste

Instructions:

1. Preheat oven to 375°F (190°C).

2. In a skillet, heat olive oil over medium heat. Add onion and cook until softened. Add ground turkey and cook until browned.

3. Stir in spinach, cooked quinoa, diced tomatoes, garlic powder, onion powder, salt, and pepper. Cook for an additional 5 minutes.

4. Stuff each bell pepper with the turkey mixture and place in a baking dish.

5. Cover with foil and bake for 30-35 minutes until peppers are tender.

6. Serve warm.

Nutritional Values (per serving):

- Protein: Supports muscle repair from ground turkey.

- Fiber: Promotes digestion from quinoa and bell peppers.

- Vitamins: Enhance immune function from spinach and bell peppers.

Grilled Salmon with Avocado Salsa

Ingredients:

- 4 salmon fillets

- 2 tablespoons olive oil

- Salt and pepper to taste

- 2 avocados, diced

- 1/4 cup red onion, finely chopped

- 1/4 cup cilantro, chopped

- 1 lime, juiced

- 1 jalapeño, seeded and chopped

Instructions:

1. Preheat grill to medium-high heat. Brush salmon fillets with olive oil and season with salt and pepper.

2. Grill salmon for 4-5 minutes per side or until cooked through.

3. In a bowl, combine diced avocados, red onion, cilantro, lime juice, and jalapeño. Mix gently.

4. Serve grilled salmon topped with avocado salsa.

Nutritional Values (per serving):

- Omega-3 fatty acids: Promote heart health from salmon.

- Healthy fats: Support brain function from avocado.

- Antioxidants: Enhance overall health from cilantro and red onion.

Vegetable Stir Fry with Tofu

Ingredients:

- 1 block firm tofu, cubed

- 1 cup broccoli florets

- 1 bell pepper, sliced

- 1 carrot, julienned

- 1/2 cup snow peas

- 2 tablespoons soy sauce

- 1 tablespoon sesame oil

- 1 garlic clove, minced

- 1 tablespoon ginger, grated

- 2 tablespoons vegetable oil

Instructions:

1. Heat vegetable oil in a large skillet over medium-high heat. Add cubed tofu and cook until golden brown on all sides.

2. Remove tofu from skillet and set aside. In the same skillet, add sesame oil and sauté garlic and ginger until fragrant.

3. Add broccoli, bell pepper, carrot, and snow peas. Stir-fry until vegetables are tender-crisp.

4. Return tofu to skillet and add soy sauce. Toss to combine and heat through.

5. Serve hot.

Nutritional Values (per serving):

- Protein: Supports muscle repair from tofu.

- Vitamins: Enhance immune function from mixed vegetables.

- Antioxidants: Protect against free radicals from ginger.

Chicken Avocado Lime Soup

Ingredients:

- 1 pound chicken breast, cooked and shredded

- 4 cups chicken broth

- 2 avocados, diced

- 1 lime, juiced

- 1 cup tomatoes, chopped

- 1/2 cup cilantro, chopped

- 2 garlic cloves, minced

- 1 tablespoon olive oil

- Salt and pepper to taste

Instructions:

1. In a large pot, heat olive oil over medium heat. Add garlic and cook until fragrant.

2. Add chicken broth and bring to a simmer. Stir in shredded chicken, tomatoes, and lime juice.

3. Cook for 10 minutes, then remove from heat.

4. Add diced avocados and cilantro. Season with salt and pepper.

5. Serve hot.

Nutritional Values (per serving):

- Protein: Supports muscle repair from chicken.

- Healthy fats: Promote heart health from avocado.

- Vitamins: Enhance immune function from tomatoes and cilantro.

Low-Carb Zucchini Noodles with Pesto

Ingredients:

- 4 zucchinis, spiralized

- 1/2 cup basil pesto

- 1/4 cup Parmesan cheese, grated

- 1 tablespoon olive oil

- Salt and pepper to taste

Instructions:

1. Heat olive oil in a large skillet over medium heat. Add zucchini noodles and sauté for 2-3 minutes until slightly tender.

2. Stir in basil pesto and cook for another 2 minutes.

3. Remove from heat and toss with grated Parmesan cheese.

4. Serve immediately.

Nutritional Values (per serving):

- Vitamins: Enhance immune function from zucchini.

- Healthy fats: Promote heart health from olive oil and pesto.

- Fiber: Supports digestion from vegetables.

Spiced Lentil Soup with Kale

Ingredients:

- 1 cup lentils, rinsed

- 4 cups vegetable broth

- 2 cups kale, chopped

- 1 onion, chopped

- 2 carrots, chopped

- 2 celery stalks, chopped

- 2 garlic cloves, minced

- 1 tablespoon olive oil

- 1 teaspoon cumin

- 1 teaspoon paprika

- Salt and pepper to taste

Instructions:

1. In a large pot, heat olive oil over medium heat. Add onion, carrots, and celery, cooking until softened.

2. Add garlic, cumin, and paprika, stirring until fragrant.

3. Stir in lentils and vegetable broth. Bring to a boil, then reduce heat and simmer until lentils are tender.

4. Add chopped kale and cook for an additional 5 minutes.

5. Season with salt and pepper before serving.

Nutritional Values (per serving):

- Protein: Supports muscle repair from lentils.

- Fiber: Promotes digestion from lentils and kale.

- Antioxidants: Enhance overall health from kale and spices.

Beef and Broccoli Stir Fry

Ingredients:

- 1 pound beef sirloin, thinly sliced

- 1 cup broccoli florets

- 1/2 cup bell pepper, sliced

- 2 garlic cloves, minced

- 1 tablespoon ginger, grated

- 1/4 cup soy sauce

- 2 tablespoons oyster sauce

- 1 tablespoon sesame oil

- 2 tablespoons vegetable oil

Instructions:

1. Heat vegetable oil in a large skillet over medium-high heat. Add sliced beef and cook until browned. Remove from skillet and set aside.

2. In the same skillet, add sesame oil and sauté garlic and ginger until fragrant.

3. Add broccoli and bell pepper, stir-frying until tender-crisp.

4. Return beef to the skillet and stir in soy sauce and oyster sauce. Toss to combine and heat through.

5. Serve hot.

Nutritional Values (per serving):

- Protein: Supports muscle repair from beef.

- Vitamins: Enhance immune function from broccoli and bell pepper.

- Antioxidants: Protect against free radicals from ginger.

Shrimp and Cucumber Salad

Ingredients:

- 1 -pound cooked shrimp, peeled and deveined

- 2 cucumbers, sliced

- 1/4 cup red onion, finely chopped

- 1/4 cup cilantro, chopped

- 1 lime, juiced

- 2 tablespoons olive oil

- Salt and pepper to taste

Instructions:

1. In a large bowl, combine cooked shrimp, sliced cucumbers, red onion, and cilantro.

2. In a small bowl, whisk together lime juice, olive oil, salt, and pepper. Pour over salad and toss to coat.

3. Serve chilled.

Nutritional Values (per serving):

- Protein: Supports muscle repair from shrimp.

- Vitamins: Enhance immune function from cucumber and cilantro.

- Healthy fats: Promote heart health from olive oil.

Stuffed Acorn Squash with Quinoa and Cranberries

Ingredients:

- 2 acorn squash, halved and seeds removed

- 1 cup cooked quinoa

- 1/2 cup dried cranberries

- 1/4 cup chopped walnuts

- 1/4 cup chopped parsley

- 1 tablespoon olive oil

- Salt and pepper to taste

Instructions:

1. Preheat oven to 375°F (190°C). Brush acorn squash halves with olive oil and season with salt and pepper. Place cut-side down on a baking sheet and roast for 30-35 minutes until tender.

2. In a bowl, combine cooked quinoa, dried cranberries, chopped walnuts, and parsley. Season with salt and pepper.

3. Fill each squash half with the quinoa mixture and serve warm.

Nutritional Values (per serving):

- Protein: Supports muscle repair from quinoa.

- Fiber: Promotes digestion from quinoa and squash.

- Antioxidants: Enhance overall health from cranberries and parsley.

Turkey Meatball Spinach Tortellini Soup

Ingredients:

- 1 pound ground turkey

- 1/2 cup breadcrumbs

- 1 egg

- 1 teaspoon garlic powder

- 1 teaspoon onion powder

- 4 cups chicken broth

- 2 cups spinach, chopped

- 1 package cheese tortellini

- 1 tablespoon olive oil

- Salt and pepper to taste

Instructions:

1. In a bowl, combine ground turkey, breadcrumbs, egg, garlic powder, onion powder, salt, and pepper. Form into small meatballs.

2. In a large pot, heat olive oil over medium heat. Add meatballs and cook until browned on all sides.

3. Add chicken broth and bring to a simmer. Stir in tortellini and cook until tender.

4. Add chopped spinach and cook for an additional 5 minutes.

5. Serve hot.

Nutritional Values (per serving):

- Protein: Supports muscle repair from turkey meatballs.

- Fiber: Promotes digestion from spinach and tortellini.

- Vitamins: Enhance immune function from spinach.

Roasted Vegetable and Hummus Wrap

Ingredients:

- 1 zucchini, sliced

- 1 red bell pepper, sliced

- 1 yellow bell pepper, sliced

- 1 red onion, sliced

- 2 tablespoons olive oil

- Salt and pepper to taste

- 4 whole grain tortillas

- 1 cup hummus

- 1/4 cup feta cheese, crumbled

Instructions:

1. Preheat oven to 400°F (200°C). Toss zucchini, bell peppers, and red onion with olive oil, salt, and pepper. Spread on a baking sheet and roast for 20-25 minutes until tender.

2. Spread hummus on each tortilla and top with roasted vegetables.

3. Sprinkle with crumbled feta cheese and roll up the tortillas.

4. Serve immediately.

Nutritional Values (per serving):

- Fiber: Promotes digestion from whole grain tortillas and vegetables.

- Protein: Supports muscle repair from hummus.
- Vitamins: Enhance immune function from mixed vegetables.

Spinach and Mushroom Quiche

Ingredients:

- 1 pie crust
- 1 cup spinach, chopped
- 1 cup mushrooms, sliced
- 1 cup shredded cheese
- 4 eggs
- 1 cup milk
- 1 tablespoon olive oil
- Salt and pepper to taste

Instructions:

1. Preheat oven to 375°F (190°C). In a skillet, heat olive oil over medium heat. Add mushrooms and cook until tender. Add spinach and cook until wilted.

2. In a bowl, whisk together eggs, milk, salt, and pepper. Stir in shredded cheese, cooked mushrooms, and spinach.

3. Pour mixture into pie crust and bake for 30-35 minutes until set.

4. Let cool slightly before serving.

Nutritional Values (per serving):

- Protein: Supports muscle repair from eggs and cheese.

- Fiber: Promotes digestion from spinach and mushrooms.
- Calcium: Supports bone health from cheese.

Lentil and Sweet Potato Chili

Ingredients:

- 1 cup lentils, rinsed
- 1 large sweet potato, peeled and diced
- 1 onion, chopped
- 2 garlic cloves, minced
- 1 bell pepper, chopped
- 1 can diced tomatoes
- 4 cups vegetable broth
- 2 tablespoons chili powder
- 1 tablespoon cumin
- 1 tablespoon olive oil
- Salt and pepper to taste

Instructions:

1. In a large pot, heat olive oil over medium heat. Add onion, garlic, and bell pepper, cooking until softened.

2. Stir in chili powder and cumin, cooking until fragrant.

3. Add lentils, diced sweet potato, diced tomatoes, and vegetable broth. Bring to a boil, then reduce heat and simmer until lentils and sweet potatoes are tender.

4. Season with salt and pepper before serving.

Nutritional Values (per serving):

- Protein: Supports muscle repair from lentils.

- Fiber: Promotes digestion from lentils and sweet potatoes.

- Vitamins: Enhance immune function from vegetables.

Grilled Portobello Mushrooms with Herbed Cheese

Ingredients:

- 4 large Portobello mushrooms, stems removed

- 1/4 cup olive oil

- 1 garlic clove, minced

- 1 teaspoon dried thyme

- 1/2 cup herbed cheese (like Boursin)

Instructions:

1. Preheat grill to medium-high heat. In a bowl, combine olive oil, minced garlic, and dried thyme.

2. Brush Portobello mushrooms with the olive oil mixture and season with salt and pepper.

3. Grill mushrooms for 4-5 minutes per side until tender.

4. Remove from grill and spread herbed cheese on the gill side of each mushroom.

5. Serve immediately.

Nutritional Values (per serving):

- Vitamins: Enhance immune function from mushrooms.

- Healthy fats: Promote heart health from olive oil.

- Protein: Supports muscle repair from herbed cheese.

Chicken Cobb Salad

Ingredients:

- 2 boneless, skinless chicken breasts

- 4 cups mixed greens

- 1 avocado, diced

- 2 hard-boiled eggs, chopped

- 1/4 cup blue cheese, crumbled

- 1/4 cup cooked bacon, crumbled

- 1/2 cup cherry tomatoes, halved

- 1/4 cup red onion, sliced

- 1/4 cup balsamic vinaigrette

- Salt and pepper to taste

Instructions:

1. Season chicken breasts with salt and pepper. Grill over medium heat until cooked through, about 6-7 minutes per side.

2. Let chicken rest for 5 minutes, then slice into strips.

3. In a large bowl, combine mixed greens, avocado, hard-boiled eggs, blue cheese, bacon, cherry tomatoes, and red onion.

4. Top with grilled chicken slices and drizzle with balsamic vinaigrette.

5. Serve immediately.

Nutritional Values (per serving):

- Protein: Supports muscle repair from chicken and eggs.

- Healthy fats: Promote heart health from avocado and blue cheese.

- Vitamins: Enhance immune function from mixed greens and tomatoes.

Seared Tuna Salad with Mixed Greens

Ingredients:

- 2 tuna steaks

- 4 cups mixed greens

- 1 avocado, sliced

- 1/2 cup cherry tomatoes, halved

- 1/4 cup red onion, sliced

- 1/4 cup cucumber, sliced

- 2 tablespoons olive oil

- 1 lime, juiced

- Salt and pepper to taste

Instructions:

1. Season tuna steaks with salt and pepper. Heat olive oil in a skillet over medium-high heat and sear tuna for 2-3 minutes per side.

2. Let tuna rest for a few minutes, then slice thinly.

3. In a large bowl, combine mixed greens, avocado, cherry tomatoes, red onion, and cucumber.

4. Top with seared tuna slices and drizzle with lime juice.

5. Serve immediately.

Nutritional Values (per serving):

- Omega-3 fatty acids: Promote heart health from tuna.

- Healthy fats: Support brain function from avocado.

- Vitamins: Enhance immune function from mixed greens and vegetables.

Eggplant and Chickpea Stew

Ingredients:

- 1 large eggplant, diced

- 1 can chickpeas, drained and rinsed

- 1 onion, chopped

- 2 garlic cloves, minced

- 1 can diced tomatoes

- 2 cups vegetable broth

- 1 teaspoon cumin

- 1 teaspoon paprika

- 1 tablespoon olive oil

- Salt and pepper to taste

Instructions:

1. In a large pot, heat olive oil over medium heat. Add onion and garlic, cooking until softened.

2. Stir in cumin and paprika, cooking until fragrant.

3. Add diced eggplant, chickpeas, diced tomatoes, and vegetable broth. Bring to a boil, then reduce heat and simmer until eggplant is tender.

4. Season with salt and pepper before serving.

Nutritional Values (per serving):

- Protein: Supports muscle repair from chickpeas.

- Fiber: Promotes digestion from chickpeas and eggplant.
- Antioxidants: Enhance overall health from tomatoes and spices.

Kale and Apple Salad with Walnuts

Ingredients:

- 4 cups kale, chopped
- 1 apple, thinly sliced
- 1/4 cup walnuts, chopped
- 1/4 cup feta cheese, crumbled
- 2 tablespoons olive oil
- 1 tablespoon apple cider vinegar
- Salt and pepper to taste

Instructions:

1. In a large bowl, combine chopped kale, sliced apple, chopped walnuts, and crumbled feta cheese.
2. In a small bowl, whisk together olive oil, apple cider vinegar, salt, and pepper. Pour over salad and toss to coat.
3. Serve immediately.

Nutritional Values (per serving):

- Vitamins: Enhance immune function from kale and apple.
- Healthy fats: Promote heart health from walnuts and olive oil.
- Protein: Supports muscle repair from feta cheese.

Spicy Chicken and Quinoa Bowl

Ingredients:

- 1 pound chicken breast, cooked and shredded
- 1 cup quinoa, cooked
- 1/2 cup black beans, drained and rinsed
- 1/2 cup corn kernels
- 1 avocado, diced
- 1/4 cup salsa
- 1/4 cup cilantro, chopped
- 1 lime, juiced
- 1 teaspoon chili powder
- Salt and pepper to taste

Instructions:

1. In a large bowl, combine shredded chicken, cooked quinoa, black beans, corn, avocado, salsa, cilantro, lime juice, and chili powder. Mix well.
2. Season with salt and pepper to taste.
3. Serve immediately.

Nutritional Values (per serving):

- Protein: Supports muscle repair from chicken and quinoa.
- Fiber: Promotes digestion from quinoa and black beans.
- Healthy fats: Promote heart health from avocado.

Vegetarian Black Bean Enchiladas

Ingredients:

- 8 corn tortillas
- 2 cups black beans, cooked and mashed
- 1 cup corn kernels
- 1 cup shredded cheese
- 1 can enchilada sauce
- 1/4 cup red onion, chopped
- 1/4 cup cilantro, chopped
- 1 tablespoon olive oil
- Salt and pepper to taste

Instructions:

1. Preheat oven to 375°F (190°C). In a bowl, combine mashed black beans, corn, chopped red onion, cilantro, salt, and pepper.
2. Spread a thin layer of enchilada sauce on the bottom of a baking dish.
3. Fill each tortilla with the black bean mixture and roll up. Place seam-side down in the baking dish.
4. Pour remaining enchilada sauce over the top and sprinkle with shredded cheese.
5. Bake for 20-25 minutes until cheese is melted and bubbly.
6. Serve warm.

Nutritional Values (per serving):

- Protein: Supports muscle repair from black beans.
- Fiber: Promotes digestion from black beans and corn.
- Vitamins: Enhance immune function from vegetables.

Asparagus and Lemon Risotto

Ingredients:

- 1 cup Arborio rice
- 1 cup asparagus, chopped
- 1/4 cup Parmesan cheese, grated
- 1/4 cup white wine
- 4 cups vegetable broth
- 1 shallot, finely chopped
- 1 garlic clove, minced
- 2 tablespoons olive oil
- 1 lemon, juiced and zested
- Salt and pepper to taste

Instructions:

1. In a saucepan, heat vegetable broth and keep it warm. In a large skillet, heat olive oil over medium heat. Add the finely chopped shallot and minced garlic, cooking until they are softened and fragrant.
2. Stir in the Arborio rice and cook for 1-2 minutes until it is lightly toasted and well-coated with oil.
3. Pour in the white wine and cook until it is mostly absorbed by the rice. Begin adding the warm vegetable broth one ladle at a time, stirring constantly and allowing the liquid to be absorbed before adding more.

4. When the rice is almost tender, stir in the chopped asparagus, lemon juice, and lemon zest. Continue to cook until the asparagus is tender and the rice is creamy.

5. Remove the skillet from the heat and stir in the grated Parmesan cheese. Season with salt and pepper to taste.

6. Serve the risotto warm, garnished with extra lemon zest or Parmesan if desired.

Nutritional Values (per serving):

- Protein: Supports muscle repair from Parmesan cheese.

- Vitamins: Enhance immune function from asparagus and lemon.

- Healthy fats: Promote heart health from olive oil.

Smoked Turkey and Collard Greens Wrap

Ingredients:

- 4 large collard green leaves

- 8 slices smoked turkey breast

- 1 avocado, sliced

- 1/4 cup shredded carrots

- 1/4 cup hummus

- 1/4 cup red bell pepper, sliced

Instructions:

1. Spread a thin layer of hummus evenly across each collard green leaf.

2. Layer each leaf with smoked turkey breast slices, ensuring an even distribution for balanced flavor in each bite.

3. Add slices of avocado, shredded carrots, and sliced red bell pepper on top of the turkey.

4. Carefully roll up each collard green leaf tightly, folding in the sides as you go to secure the ingredients within the wrap.

5. Slice each wrap in half for easier handling and presentation.

6. Serve immediately, enjoying the fresh, crisp texture and savory flavors.

Nutritional Values (per serving):

- Protein: Supports muscle repair from smoked turkey.

- Healthy fats: Promote heart health from avocado.

- Fiber: Supports digestion from collard greens and vegetables.

DINNER

Lemon Garlic Baked Cod

Ingredients:

- 4 cod fillets
- 2 tablespoons olive oil
- 2 garlic cloves, minced
- 1 lemon, sliced into rounds
- 1/4 cup fresh parsley, chopped
- Salt and pepper to taste

Instructions:

1. Preheat oven to 375°F (190°C). Grease a baking dish with olive oil.

2. Place cod fillets in the baking dish. Drizzle with olive oil and sprinkle with minced garlic, salt, and pepper.

3. Lay lemon slices on top of the cod and bake for 20-25 minutes or until the fish flakes easily with a fork.

4. Garnish with fresh parsley before serving.

Nutritional Values (per serving):

- Protein: Supports muscle repair from cod.
- Healthy fats: Promote heart health from olive oil.
- Antioxidants: Enhance overall health from garlic and parsley.

Chicken Parmesan with Zucchini Noodles

Ingredients:

- 2 boneless, skinless chicken breasts
- 1 cup marinara sauce
- 1/2 cup mozzarella cheese, shredded
- 1/4 cup Parmesan cheese, grated
- 2 zucchinis, spiralized into noodles
- 1/4 cup almond flour
- 1 egg, beaten
- 2 tablespoons olive oil
- Salt and pepper to taste

Instructions:

1. Preheat oven to 375°F (190°C). Season chicken breasts with salt and pepper.

2. Dredge chicken in beaten egg, then coat with almond flour.

3. Heat olive oil in a skillet over medium heat. Cook chicken until golden brown on both sides.

4. Place chicken in a baking dish, top with marinara sauce, mozzarella, and Parmesan cheese. Bake for 20-25 minutes until chicken is cooked through.

5. While chicken is baking, sauté zucchini noodles in a separate skillet for 2-3 minutes.

6. Serve chicken Parmesan over zucchini noodles.

Nutritional Values (per serving):

- Protein: Supports muscle repair from chicken and cheese.

- Vitamins: Enhance immune function from zucchini.

- Healthy fats: Promote heart health from olive oil.

Beef Stir Fry with Mixed Vegetables

Ingredients:

- 1 pound beef sirloin, thinly sliced

- 2 cups broccoli florets

- 1 bell pepper, sliced

- 1 carrot, julienned

- 1/2 cup snap peas

- 2 tablespoons soy sauce

- 1 tablespoon oyster sauce

- 1 tablespoon sesame oil

- 2 garlic cloves, minced

- 1 tablespoon vegetable oil

- Salt and pepper to taste

Instructions:

1. Heat vegetable oil in a large skillet over medium-high heat. Add sliced beef and cook until browned. Remove from skillet and set aside.

2. In the same skillet, add sesame oil and sauté garlic until fragrant.

3. Add broccoli, bell pepper, carrot, and snap peas. Stir-fry until vegetables are tender-crisp.

4. Return beef to the skillet and add soy sauce and oyster sauce. Toss to combine and heat through.

5. Serve hot.

Nutritional Values (per serving):

- Protein: Supports muscle repair from beef.

- Vitamins: Enhance immune function from mixed vegetables.

- Antioxidants: Protect against free radicals from vegetables.

Pork Tenderloin with Applesauce

Ingredients:

- 1 pork tenderloin

- 1 cup unsweetened applesauce

- 1 tablespoon Dijon mustard

- 1 tablespoon honey

- 1/2 teaspoon cinnamon

- Salt and pepper to taste

Instructions:

1. Preheat oven to 375°F (190°C). Season pork tenderloin with salt and pepper.

2. In a bowl, mix applesauce, Dijon mustard, honey, and cinnamon.

3. Place pork tenderloin in a baking dish and spread applesauce mixture over the top.

4. Bake for 25-30 minutes or until the pork reaches an internal temperature of 145°F (63°C).

5. Let rest for 5 minutes before slicing and serving.

Nutritional Values (per serving):

- Protein: Supports muscle repair from pork.

- Vitamins: Enhance immune function from applesauce.

- Healthy fats: Provide satiety from the pork tenderloin.

Vegetarian Moussaka

Ingredients:

- 2 large eggplants, sliced

- 1 onion, chopped

- 2 garlic cloves, minced

- 1 can lentils, drained and rinsed

- 1 can diced tomatoes

- 1 teaspoon cinnamon

- 1 teaspoon oregano

- 1 cup ricotta cheese

- 1/2 cup Parmesan cheese, grated

- 1 egg, beaten

- 2 tablespoons olive oil

- Salt and pepper to taste

Instructions:

1. Preheat oven to 375°F (190°C). Brush eggplant slices with olive oil and roast for 20 minutes until tender.

2. In a skillet, heat olive oil over medium heat. Add onion and garlic, cooking until softened.

3. Stir in lentils, diced tomatoes, cinnamon, and oregano. Cook for 10 minutes.

4. In a bowl, mix ricotta cheese, Parmesan cheese, and beaten egg.

5. In a baking dish, layer eggplant slices, lentil mixture, and ricotta mixture. Repeat layers.

6. Bake for 30-35 minutes until golden and bubbling. Serve warm.

Nutritional Values (per serving):

- Protein: Supports muscle repair from lentils and cheese.

- Fiber: Promotes digestion from lentils and eggplant.

- Antioxidants: Enhance overall health from tomatoes and spices.

Balsamic Glazed Salmon

Ingredients:

- 4 salmon fillets

- 1/4 cup balsamic vinegar

- 2 tablespoons honey

- 2 garlic cloves, minced

- 1 tablespoon olive oil

- Salt and pepper to taste

Instructions:

1. Preheat oven to 400°F (200°C). In a small bowl, whisk together balsamic vinegar, honey, and minced garlic.

2. Place salmon fillets on a baking sheet lined with parchment paper. Drizzle with olive oil and season with salt and pepper.

3. Brush balsamic glaze over the salmon fillets.

4. Bake for 12-15 minutes or until salmon is cooked through.

5. Serve immediately, garnished with extra glaze if desired.

Nutritional Values (per serving):

- Omega-3 fatty acids: Promote heart health from salmon.

- Healthy fats: Support brain function from olive oil.

- Antioxidants: Enhance overall health from balsamic vinegar.

Thai Green Curry with Shrimp

Ingredients:

- 1 pound shrimp, peeled and deveined

- 1 can coconut milk

- 2 tablespoons green curry paste

- 1 bell pepper, sliced

- 1 cup snap peas

- 1 cup bamboo shoots, drained

- 1 tablespoon fish sauce

- 1 tablespoon brown sugar

- 1 lime, juiced

- 1/4 cup fresh basil, chopped

- 1 tablespoon vegetable oil

Instructions:

1. Heat vegetable oil in a large skillet over medium heat. Add green curry paste and sauté until fragrant.

2. Stir in coconut milk, fish sauce, and brown sugar. Bring to a simmer.

3. Add bell pepper, snap peas, and bamboo shoots. Cook until vegetables are tender.

4. Add shrimp and cook until pink and opaque.

5. Stir in lime juice and fresh basil before serving.

6. Serve hot with rice.

Nutritional Values (per serving):

- Protein: Supports muscle repair from shrimp.

- Healthy fats: Promote heart health from coconut milk.

- Vitamins: Enhance immune function from vegetables.

Slow Cooker Moroccan Chicken

Ingredients:

- 4 boneless, skinless chicken thighs

- 1 can chickpeas, drained and rinsed

- 1 cup chicken broth

- 1 onion, chopped

- 2 garlic cloves, minced

- 1 cup diced tomatoes

- 1/2 cup dried apricots, chopped

- 1 tablespoon honey

- 1 teaspoon ground cumin

- 1 teaspoon ground cinnamon

- 1 teaspoon ground ginger
- Salt and pepper to taste

Instructions:

1. Place chicken thighs in the slow cooker. Add chickpeas, chicken broth, onion, garlic, diced tomatoes, dried apricots, honey, cumin, cinnamon, and ginger.

2. Stir to combine and season with salt and pepper.

3. Cook on low for 6-8 hours or on high for 3-4 hours until chicken is tender and cooked through.

4. Serve hot, garnished with fresh cilantro if desired.

Nutritional Values (per serving):

- Protein: Supports muscle repair from chicken and chickpeas.
- Fiber: Promotes digestion from chickpeas.
- Antioxidants: Enhance overall health from spices and dried apricots.

Herb-Crusted Rack of Lamb

Ingredients:

- 1 rack of lamb, trimmed
- 2 tablespoons Dijon mustard
- 1/2 cup breadcrumbs
- 1/4 cup fresh parsley, chopped
- 1 tablespoon fresh rosemary, chopped
- 1 tablespoon fresh thyme, chopped
- 2 tablespoons olive oil

- Salt and pepper to taste

Instructions:

1. Preheat oven to 400°F (200°C). Season the rack of lamb with salt and pepper.

2. Brush Dijon mustard over the lamb.

3. In a bowl, mix breadcrumbs, parsley, rosemary, thyme, and olive oil.

4. Press the herb mixture onto the lamb to form a crust.

5. Place lamb in a roasting pan and roast for 20-25 minutes for medium-rare, or longer for desired doneness.

6. Let rest for 10 minutes before slicing and serving.

Nutritional Values (per serving):

- Protein: Supports muscle repair from lamb.
- Healthy fats: Promote heart health from olive oil.
- Antioxidants: Enhance overall health from fresh herbs.

Stuffed Chicken Breast with Spinach and Ricotta

Ingredients:

- 4 boneless, skinless chicken breasts
- 1 cup fresh spinach, chopped
- 1/2 cup ricotta cheese
- 1/4 cup Parmesan cheese, grated
- 2 garlic cloves, minced
- 1 tablespoon olive oil
- Salt and pepper to taste

Instructions:

1. Preheat oven to 375°F (190°C). In a bowl, mix chopped spinach, ricotta cheese, Parmesan cheese, and minced garlic.

2. Season the chicken breasts with salt and pepper. Cut a pocket into each chicken breast and stuff with the spinach and ricotta mixture.

3. Secure with toothpicks if necessary.

4. Heat olive oil in a skillet over medium-high heat. Sear the stuffed chicken breasts until golden brown on both sides.

5. Transfer chicken to a baking dish and bake for 20-25 minutes until cooked through.

6. Serve hot.

Nutritional Values (per serving):

- Protein: Supports muscle repair from chicken and ricotta.

- Vitamins: Enhance immune function from spinach.

- Healthy fats: Promote heart health from olive oil.

Butternut Squash and Black Bean Enchiladas

Ingredients:

- 8 corn tortillas

- 2 cups butternut squash, diced and roasted

- 1 can black beans, drained and rinsed

- 1 cup enchilada sauce

- 1/2 cup shredded cheese

- 1/4 cup red onion, chopped

- 1/4 cup cilantro, chopped

- 1 tablespoon olive oil

- Salt and pepper to taste

Instructions:

1. Preheat oven to 375°F (190°C). Toss butternut squash with olive oil, salt, and pepper, and roast for 25-30 minutes until tender.

2. In a bowl, combine roasted butternut squash, black beans, red onion, and cilantro.

3. Spread a thin layer of enchilada sauce on the bottom of a baking dish.

4. Fill each tortilla with the butternut squash mixture, roll up, and place seam-side down in the baking dish.

5. Pour remaining enchilada sauce over the top and sprinkle with shredded cheese.

6. Bake for 20-25 minutes until cheese is melted and bubbly. Serve warm.

Nutritional Values (per serving):

- Protein: Supports muscle repair from black beans.

- Fiber: Promotes digestion from butternut squash and beans.

- Vitamins: Enhance immune function from vegetables.

Grilled Steak with Mushroom Sauce

Ingredients:

- 4 steaks (ribeye, sirloin, or your choice)
- 2 cups mushrooms, sliced
- 1/2 cup beef broth
- 1/4 cup heavy cream
- 2 garlic cloves, minced
- 2 tablespoons olive oil
- 1 tablespoon butter
- Salt and pepper to taste

Instructions:

1. Preheat grill to medium-high heat. Season steaks with salt and pepper.

2. Grill steaks for 4-5 minutes per side or until desired doneness. Let rest for 5 minutes.

3. In a skillet, heat olive oil and butter over medium heat. Add minced garlic and cook until fragrant.

4. Add sliced mushrooms and sauté until tender.

5. Stir in beef broth and heavy cream. Cook until the sauce thickens.

6. Serve steaks topped with mushroom sauce.

Nutritional Values (per serving):

- Protein: Supports muscle repair from steak.
- Healthy fats: Promote heart health from olive oil and butter.
- Vitamins: Enhance immune function from mushrooms.

Tofu Tikka Masala

Ingredients:

- 1 block firm tofu, cubed
- 1 onion, chopped
- 2 garlic cloves, minced
- 1 tablespoon ginger, grated
- 1 can diced tomatoes
- 1 cup coconut milk
- 2 tablespoons tikka masala paste
- 1 tablespoon vegetable oil
- 1 teaspoon cumin
- 1 teaspoon coriander
- Salt and pepper to taste

Instructions:

1. Heat vegetable oil in a large skillet over medium heat. Add cubed tofu and cook until golden brown on all sides. Remove from skillet and set aside.

2. In the same skillet, add onion, garlic, and ginger, cooking until softened.

3. Stir in tikka masala paste, cumin, and coriander, cooking until fragrant.

4. Add diced tomatoes and coconut milk. Bring to a simmer.

5. Return tofu to the skillet and cook until heated through.

6. Serve hot with rice or naan.

Nutritional Values (per serving):

- Protein: Supports muscle repair from tofu.

- Healthy fats: Promote heart health from coconut milk.

- Antioxidants: Enhance overall health from spices and tomatoes.

Baked Tilapia with Tomato and Basil

Ingredients:

- 4 tilapia fillets

- 2 cups cherry tomatoes, halved

- 1/4 cup fresh basil, chopped

- 2 garlic cloves, minced

- 2 tablespoons olive oil

- Salt and pepper to taste

Instructions:

1. Preheat oven to 375°F (190°C). Place tilapia fillets in a baking dish.

2. In a bowl, combine cherry tomatoes, fresh basil, minced garlic, olive oil, salt, and pepper.

3. Spoon the tomato mixture over the tilapia fillets.

4. Bake for 20-25 minutes until the fish flakes easily with a fork.

5. Serve immediately.

Nutritional Values (per serving):

- Protein: Supports muscle repair from tilapia.

- Healthy fats: Promote heart health from olive oil.

- Antioxidants: Enhance overall health from tomatoes and basil.

Pork Chops with Apple Cider Glaze

Ingredients:

- 4 pork chops

- 1 cup apple cider

- 1/4 cup apple cider vinegar

- 2 tablespoons brown sugar

- 1 tablespoon Dijon mustard

- 1 tablespoon olive oil

- Salt and pepper to taste

Instructions:

1. Season pork chops with salt and pepper. Heat olive oil in a skillet over medium-high heat and sear pork chops until golden brown on both sides. Remove and set aside.

2. In the same skillet, add apple cider, apple cider vinegar, brown sugar, and Dijon mustard. Bring to a boil, then reduce heat and simmer until the glaze thickens.

3. Return pork chops to the skillet, coating them with the glaze. Cook until pork chops are cooked through.

4. Serve hot, drizzled with additional glaze.

Nutritional Values (per serving):

- Protein: Supports muscle repair from pork chops.

- Vitamins: Enhance immune function from apple cider.

- Healthy fats: Promote heart health from olive oil.

Vegan Shepherd's Pie

Ingredients:

- 4 large potatoes, peeled and chopped
- 1 cup lentils, cooked
- 1 onion, chopped
- 2 carrots, diced
- 2 celery stalks, diced
- 1 cup peas
- 1 cup corn
- 1 can diced tomatoes
- 1 tablespoon olive oil
- 1 teaspoon thyme
- 1 teaspoon rosemary
- Salt and pepper to taste

Instructions:

1. Preheat oven to 375°F (190°C). Boil potatoes until tender, then mash and season with salt and pepper.

2. In a skillet, heat olive oil over medium heat. Add onion, carrots, and celery, cooking until softened.

3. Stir in cooked lentils, diced tomatoes, thyme, rosemary, salt, and pepper. Cook until heated through.

4. Transfer lentil mixture to a baking dish and spread mashed potatoes on top.

5. Bake for 20-25 minutes until the top is golden brown.

6. Serve hot.

Nutritional Values (per serving):

- Protein: Supports muscle repair from lentils.
- Fiber: Promotes digestion from vegetables and lentils.
- Vitamins: Enhance immune function from mixed vegetables.

Turkey Chili

Ingredients:

- 1 pound ground turkey
- 1 onion, chopped
- 2 garlic cloves, minced
- 1 bell pepper, chopped
- 1 can kidney beans, drained and rinsed
- 1 can diced tomatoes
- 2 tablespoons chili powder
- 1 teaspoon cumin
- 1 teaspoon paprika
- 1 tablespoon olive oil
- Salt and pepper to taste

Instructions:

1. Heat olive oil in a large pot over medium heat. Add onion and garlic, cooking until softened.

2. Add ground turkey and cook until browned.

3. Stir in bell pepper, kidney beans, diced tomatoes, chili powder, cumin, and paprika. Bring to a simmer.

4. Cook for 30 minutes, stirring occasionally. Season with salt and pepper.

5. Serve hot, garnished with fresh cilantro if desired.

Nutritional Values (per serving):

- Protein: Supports muscle repair from ground turkey.

- Fiber: Promotes digestion from kidney beans.

- Antioxidants: Enhance overall health from spices and vegetables.

Grilled Mahi with Tropical Salsa

Ingredients:

- 4 Mahi fillets

- 1 mango, diced

- 1 avocado, diced

- 1/2 red onion, finely chopped

- 1/4 cup cilantro, chopped

- 1 lime, juiced

- 1 tablespoon olive oil

- Salt and pepper to taste

Instructions:

1. Preheat grill to medium-high heat. Season Mahi fillets with salt and pepper and drizzle with olive oil.

2. Grill Mahi for 4-5 minutes per side until cooked through.

3. In a bowl, combine diced mango, avocado, red onion, cilantro, and lime juice. Mix gently.

4. Serve grilled Mahi topped with tropical salsa.

Nutritional Values (per serving):

- Protein: Supports muscle repair from Mahi.

- Healthy fats: Promote heart health from avocado and olive oil.

- Vitamins: Enhance immune function from mango and lime.

Roasted Duck with Orange Sauce

Ingredients:

- 1 whole duck

- 1 cup orange juice

- 1/4 cup honey

- 2 tablespoons soy sauce

- 1 tablespoon ginger, grated

- Salt and pepper to taste

Instructions:

1. Preheat oven to 375°F (190°C). Season duck with salt and pepper.

2. In a small bowl, combine orange juice, honey, soy sauce, and grated ginger.

3. Place duck on a rack in a roasting pan and brush with the orange sauce mixture.

4. Roast for 1.5-2 hours, basting with sauce every 30 minutes, until duck is cooked through and skin is crispy.

5. Let rest for 10 minutes before carving and serving.

Nutritional Values (per serving):

- Protein: Supports muscle repair from duck.

- Healthy fats: Promote heart health from duck.

- Vitamins: Enhance immune function from orange juice and ginger.

Vegetarian Paella

Ingredients:

- 1 cup Arborio rice

- 1 bell pepper, chopped

- 1 zucchini, sliced

- 1 cup peas

- 1 can diced tomatoes

- 2 cups vegetable broth

- 1 onion, chopped

- 2 garlic cloves, minced

- 1 teaspoon smoked paprika

- 1/4 teaspoon saffron threads

- 2 tablespoons olive oil

- Salt and pepper to taste

Instructions:

1. In a large skillet, heat olive oil over medium heat. Add onion and garlic, cooking until softened.

2. Stir in Arborio rice, smoked paprika, and saffron, cooking for 1-2 minutes.

3. Add vegetable broth, diced tomatoes, bell pepper, zucchini, and peas. Bring to a boil, then reduce heat and simmer until rice is tender and liquid is absorbed.

4. Season with salt and pepper before serving.

Nutritional Values (per serving):

- Protein: Supports muscle repair from peas.

- Vitamins: Enhance immune function from mixed vegetables.

- Antioxidants: Protect against free radicals from spices and vegetables.

Seared Scallops with Cauliflower Puree

Ingredients:

- 1- pound scallops

- 1 head cauliflower, chopped

- 1/2 cup heavy cream

- 2 garlic cloves, minced

- 2 tablespoons butter

- 1 tablespoon olive oil

- Salt and pepper to taste

Instructions:

1. In a pot, boil cauliflower until tender. Drain and blend with heavy cream, garlic, salt, and pepper until smooth.

2. Season scallops with salt and pepper. Heat olive oil in a skillet over medium-high heat and sear, scallops for 2-3 minutes per side until golden brown.

3. Serve scallops on a bed of cauliflower puree.

Nutritional Values (per serving):

- Protein: Supports muscle repair from scallops.

- Healthy fats: Promote heart health from olive oil and butter.

- Vitamins: Enhance immune function from cauliflower.

Beef and Vegetable Kebabs

Ingredients:

- 1 pound beef sirloin, cubed

- 1 bell pepper, chopped

- 1 zucchini, sliced

- 1 red onion, chopped

- 1/4 cup soy sauce

- 2 tablespoons olive oil

- 1 tablespoon honey

- 1 garlic clove, minced

- Salt and pepper to taste

Instructions:

1. In a bowl, combine soy sauce, olive oil, honey, minced garlic, salt, and pepper. Marinate beef cubes for at least 30 minutes.

2. Preheat grill to medium-high heat. Thread beef, bell pepper, zucchini, and red onion onto skewers.

3. Grill kebabs for 8-10 minutes, turning occasionally, until beef is cooked to desired doneness.

4. Serve hot.

Nutritional Values (per serving):

- Protein: Supports muscle repair from beef.

- Vitamins: Enhance immune function from mixed vegetables.

- Healthy fats: Promote heart health from olive oil.

Chicken and Vegetable Soup

Ingredients:

- 1 pound chicken breast, cooked and shredded

- 4 cups chicken broth

- 1 onion, chopped

- 2 carrots, sliced

- 2 celery stalks, sliced

- 1 cup peas

- 2 garlic cloves, minced

- 1 tablespoon olive oil

- Salt and pepper to taste

Instructions:

1. In a large pot, heat olive oil over medium heat. Add onion, carrots, celery, and garlic, cooking until softened.

2. Stir in chicken broth and bring to a boil.

3. Add shredded chicken and peas. Simmer for 10-15 minutes.

4. Season with salt and pepper before serving.

Nutritional Values (per serving):

- Protein: Supports muscle repair from chicken.

- Fiber: Promotes digestion from vegetables.

- Vitamins: Enhance immune function from mixed vegetables.

Spaghetti Squash with Meatballs

Ingredients:

- 1 spaghetti squash, halved and seeded

- 1 pound ground beef

- 1 egg

- 1/4 cup breadcrumbs

- 1/4 cup Parmesan cheese, grated

- 2 garlic cloves, minced

- 1 jar marinara sauce

- 2 tablespoons olive oil

- Salt and pepper to taste

Instructions:

1. Preheat oven to 375°F (190°C). Drizzle spaghetti squash halves with olive oil, salt, and pepper. Place cut-side down on a baking sheet and roast for 40 minutes until tender.

2. In a bowl, combine ground beef, egg, breadcrumbs, Parmesan cheese, minced garlic, salt, and pepper. Form into meatballs.

3. In a skillet, heat olive oil over medium heat. Cook meatballs until browned on all sides. Add marinara sauce and simmer until meatballs are cooked through.

4. Use a fork to scrape the spaghetti squash into strands. Serve meatballs and sauce over spaghetti squash.

Nutritional Values (per serving):

- Protein: Supports muscle repair from beef and cheese.

- Fiber: Promotes digestion from spaghetti squash.

- Vitamins: Enhance immune function from squash and sauce.

Rack of Lamb with Mint Pesto

Ingredients:

- 1 rack of lamb, trimmed

- 1 cup fresh mint leaves

- 1/2 cup fresh parsley

- 1/4 cup pine nuts

- 1/4 cup Parmesan cheese, grated

- 1 garlic clove, minced

- 1/4 cup olive oil

- Salt and pepper to taste

Instructions:

1. Preheat oven to 400°F (200°C). Season rack of lamb with salt and pepper.

2. In a food processor, combine mint leaves, parsley, pine nuts, Parmesan cheese, and minced garlic. Pulse until combined.

3. Slowly add olive oil while processing until a smooth pesto forms.

4. Spread mint pesto over the rack of lamb.

5. Place lamb in a roasting pan and roast for 20-25 minutes for medium-rare, or longer for desired doneness.

6. Let rest for 10 minutes before slicing and serving.

Nutritional Values (per serving):

- Protein: Supports muscle repair from lamb.

- Healthy fats: Promote heart health from olive oil and pine nuts.

- Antioxidants: Enhance overall health from fresh herbs.

SNACKS

Celery Sticks with Almond Butter

Ingredients:

- 6 celery sticks
- 1/4 cup almond butter
- 1 tablespoon raisins (optional)

Instructions:

1. Wash and trim the celery sticks.
2. Spread almond butter evenly into the grooves of the celery sticks.
3. Top with raisins if desired.
4. Serve immediately as a healthy snack.

Nutritional Values (per serving):

- Protein: Supports muscle repair from almond butter.
- Fiber: Promotes digestion from celery.
- Healthy fats: Promote heart health from almond butter.

Greek Yogurt and Honey

Ingredients:

- 1 cup Greek yogurt
- 1 tablespoon honey
- 1/4 teaspoon cinnamon (optional)

Instructions:

1. Scoop Greek yogurt into a bowl.
2. Drizzle honey over the top.
3. Sprinkle with cinnamon if desired.
4. Mix gently and enjoy.

Nutritional Values (per serving):

- Protein: Supports muscle repair from Greek yogurt.
- Probiotics: Enhance gut health from yogurt.
- Antioxidants: Improve overall health from honey and cinnamon.

Spiced Nuts

Ingredients:

- 1 cup mixed nuts (almonds, walnuts, cashews)
- 1 tablespoon olive oil
- 1 teaspoon paprika
- 1/2 teaspoon cumin
- 1/2 teaspoon chili powder
- Salt to taste

Instructions:

1. Preheat oven to 350°F (175°C).
2. In a bowl, toss mixed nuts with olive oil, paprika, cumin, chili powder, and salt.
3. Spread nuts on a baking sheet and roast for 10-12 minutes, stirring occasionally, until golden and fragrant.
4. Let cool before serving.

Nutritional Values (per serving):

- Protein: Supports muscle repair from mixed nuts.

- Healthy fats: Promote heart health from nuts.

- Antioxidants: Protect against free radicals from spices.

Cheese and Whole-Grain Crackers

Ingredients:

- 1/4 cup cheese, sliced (cheddar, gouda, or your choice)

- 10 whole-grain crackers

Instructions:

1. Slice the cheese into small pieces.

2. Arrange cheese slices on a plate with whole-grain crackers.

3. Serve as a quick and easy snack.

Nutritional Values (per serving):

- Protein: Supports muscle repair from cheese.

- Fiber: Promotes digestion from whole-grain crackers.

- Calcium: Supports bone health from cheese.

Fresh Fruit Salad

Ingredients:

- 1 cup strawberries, hulled and sliced

- 1 cup blueberries

- 1 cup pineapple, diced

- 1 cup kiwi, peeled and sliced

- 1 tablespoon lemon juice

- 1 tablespoon honey

Instructions:

1. In a large bowl, combine strawberries, blueberries, pineapple, and kiwi.

2. Drizzle with lemon juice and honey.

3. Toss gently to coat and serve immediately.

Nutritional Values (per serving):

- Vitamins: Enhance immune function from mixed fruits.

- Fiber: Promotes digestion from fruits.

- Antioxidants: Improve overall health from berries.

Kale Chips

Ingredients:

- 1 bunch kale, washed and torn into pieces

- 2 tablespoons olive oil

- Salt to taste

Instructions:

1. Preheat oven to 350°F (175°C).

2. In a bowl, toss kale pieces with olive oil and salt.

3. Spread kale on a baking sheet in a single layer.

4. Bake for 10-15 minutes until crispy, checking frequently to prevent burning.

5. Let cool before serving.

Nutritional Values (per serving):

- Vitamins: Enhance immune function from kale.
- Fiber: Promotes digestion from kale.
- Healthy fats: Promote heart health from olive oil.

Mixed Berries with Whipped Coconut Cream

Ingredients:

- 1 cup mixed berries (strawberries, blueberries, raspberries)
- 1 can coconut milk, chilled
- 1 tablespoon honey
- 1 teaspoon vanilla extract

Instructions:

1. Scoop the solid part of the chilled coconut milk into a bowl.
2. Whip the coconut cream with honey and vanilla extract until light and fluffy.
3. Serve mixed berries topped with whipped coconut cream.

Nutritional Values (per serving):

- Antioxidants: Protect against free radicals from berries.
- Healthy fats: Promote heart health from coconut milk.
- Vitamins: Enhance immune function from mixed berries.

Boiled Eggs with Spinach Dip

Ingredients:

- 4 boiled eggs, peeled
- 1 cup fresh spinach, chopped
- 1/2 cup Greek yogurt
- 1 garlic clove, minced
- 1 tablespoon lemon juice
- Salt and pepper to taste

Instructions:

1. In a bowl, combine chopped spinach, Greek yogurt, minced garlic, lemon juice, salt, and pepper.
2. Serve boiled eggs with spinach dip.

Nutritional Values (per serving):

- Protein: Supports muscle repair from eggs and yogurt.
- Vitamins: Enhance immune function from spinach.
- Probiotics: Improve gut health from yogurt.

Turkey Jerky

Ingredients:

- 1 pound turkey breast, thinly sliced
- 1/4 cup soy sauce
- 1 tablespoon honey
- 1 teaspoon black pepper
- 1 teaspoon garlic powder

Instructions:

1. Marinate turkey slices in soy sauce, honey, black pepper, and garlic powder for at least 2 hours.

2. Preheat oven to 175°F (80°C). Place turkey slices on a wire rack over a baking sheet.

3. Dry in the oven for 4-6 hours until jerky is dry but still pliable.

4. Let cool before storing in an airtight container.

Nutritional Values (per serving):

- Protein: Supports muscle repair from turkey.

- Low-fat: Helps maintain lean body mass from turkey breast.

- Flavorful: Natural seasonings provide a satisfying taste.

Low-Carb Cheese Puffs

Ingredients:

- 1 cup shredded cheddar cheese

- 1/2 cup almond flour

- 1 egg

- 1/2 teaspoon baking powder

- 1/4 teaspoon garlic powder

- Salt to taste

Instructions:

1. Preheat oven to 350°F (175°C).

2. In a bowl, mix shredded cheddar cheese, almond flour, egg, baking powder, garlic powder, and salt until well combined.

3. Scoop small portions of the mixture onto a baking sheet lined with parchment paper.

4. Bake for 10-12 minutes until golden and puffed.

5. Let cool before serving.

Nutritional Values (per serving):

- Protein: Supports muscle repair from cheese and egg.

- Low-carb: Suitable for ketogenic diets.

- Healthy fats: Promote satiety from almond flour.

Zucchini and Carrot Fritters

Ingredients:

- 1 zucchini, grated

- 1 carrot, grated

- 1/4 cup almond flour

- 1 egg

- 1 garlic clove, minced

- 2 tablespoons olive oil

- Salt and pepper to taste

Instructions:

1. In a bowl, combine grated zucchini, grated carrot, almond flour, egg, minced garlic, salt, and pepper.

2. Heat olive oil in a skillet over medium heat. Scoop small portions of the mixture into the skillet and flatten slightly.

3. Cook until golden brown on both sides, about 3-4 minutes per side.

4. Drain on paper towels before serving.

Nutritional Values (per serving):

- Vitamins: Enhance immune function from zucchini and carrot.

- Fiber: Promotes digestion from vegetables.

- Healthy fats: Promote heart health from olive oil.

Baked Apple Chips

Ingredients:

- 2 apples, thinly sliced

- 1 teaspoon cinnamon

- 1 tablespoon honey

Instructions:

1. Preheat oven to 225°F (110°C). Line a baking sheet with parchment paper.

2. Arrange apple slices in a single layer on the baking sheet. Drizzle with honey and sprinkle with cinnamon.

3. Bake for 1.5-2 hours, flipping halfway, until crisp.

4. Let cool before serving.

Nutritional Values (per serving):

- Fiber: Promotes digestion from apples.

- Antioxidants: Enhance overall health from cinnamon.

- Natural sweetness: Satisfies sweet cravings from honey and apples.

Avocado Chocolate Mousse

Ingredients:

- 2 ripe avocados

- 1/4 cup cocoa powder

- 1/4 cup maple syrup

- 1 teaspoon vanilla extract

- Pinch of salt

Instructions:

1. In a blender, combine avocados, cocoa powder, maple syrup, vanilla extract, and a pinch of salt. Blend until smooth and creamy.

2. Chill for at least 30 minutes before serving.

Nutritional Values (per serving):

- Healthy fats: Promote heart health from avocados.

- Antioxidants: Enhance overall health from cocoa powder.

- Natural sweetness: Satisfies sweet cravings from maple syrup.

Roasted Chickpeas

Ingredients:

- 1 can chickpeas, drained and rinsed

- 1 tablespoon olive oil

- 1 teaspoon smoked paprika

- 1/2 teaspoon garlic powder

- Salt to taste

Instructions:

1. Preheat oven to 400°F (200°C). Pat chickpeas dry with a paper towel.

2. In a bowl, toss chickpeas with olive oil, smoked paprika, garlic powder, and salt.

3. Spread chickpeas on a baking sheet in a single layer.

4. Roast for 20-25 minutes until crispy, shaking the pan occasionally.

5. Let cool before serving.

Nutritional Values (per serving):

- Protein: Supports muscle repair from chickpeas.

- Fiber: Promotes digestion from chickpeas.

- Antioxidants: Enhance overall health from spices.

Cucumber and Hummus Bites

Ingredients:

- 1 cucumber, sliced into rounds

- 1/2 cup hummus

- 1 tablespoon fresh dill, chopped (optional)

Instructions:

1. Arrange cucumber slices on a serving platter.

2. Spoon a small amount of hummus onto each cucumber slice.

3. Garnish with fresh dill if desired.

4. Serve immediately.

Nutritional Values (per serving):

- Fiber: Promotes digestion from cucumber.

- Protein: Supports muscle repair from hummus.

- Vitamins: Enhance immune function from cucumber and dill.

Coconut Yogurt with Walnuts and Cinnamon

Ingredients:

- 1 cup coconut yogurt

- 1/4 cup walnuts, chopped

- 1 teaspoon cinnamon

- 1 tablespoon honey (optional)

Instructions:

1. Scoop coconut yogurt into a bowl.

2. Top with chopped walnuts and sprinkle with cinnamon.

3. Drizzle with honey if desired.

4. Mix gently and enjoy.

Nutritional Values (per serving):

- Healthy fats: Promote heart health from walnuts and coconut yogurt.

- Fiber: Promotes digestion from walnuts.

- Antioxidants: Enhance overall health from cinnamon.

Protein Balls with Oats and Peanut Butter

Ingredients:

- 1 cup rolled oats

- 1/2 cup peanut butter

- 1/4 cup honey

- 1/4 cup protein powder

- 1 teaspoon vanilla extract

Instructions:

1. In a bowl, combine rolled oats, peanut butter, honey, protein powder, and vanilla extract.

2. Mix until well combined. Roll mixture into small balls.

3. Chill for at least 30 minutes before serving.

Nutritional Values (per serving):

- Protein: Supports muscle repair from peanut butter and protein powder.

- Fiber: Promotes digestion from oats.

- Healthy fats: Provide satiety from peanut butter.

Stuffed Dates with Goat Cheese

Ingredients:

- 12 Medjool dates, pitted

- 1/4 cup goat cheese

- 1 tablespoon honey

- 1/4 teaspoon cinnamon

Instructions:

1. In a bowl, mix goat cheese, honey, and cinnamon.

2. Stuff each date with the goat cheese mixture.

3. Serve immediately as a sweet and savory snack.

Nutritional Values (per serving):

- Fiber: Promotes digestion from dates.

- Protein: Supports muscle repair from goat cheese.

- Vitamins: Enhance immune function from dates.

Almond and Flax Seed Granola

Ingredients:

- 2 cups rolled oats

- 1/2 cup almonds, chopped

- 1/4 cup flax seeds

- 1/4 cup honey

- 2 tablespoons coconut oil

- 1 teaspoon vanilla extract

- 1/2 teaspoon cinnamon

Instructions:

1. Preheat oven to 300°F (150°C). In a bowl, mix rolled oats, chopped almonds, flax seeds, honey, coconut oil, vanilla extract, and cinnamon.

2. Spread mixture on a baking sheet lined with parchment paper.

3. Bake for 20-25 minutes, stirring occasionally, until golden brown.

4. Let cool before serving.

Nutritional Values (per serving):

- Fiber: Promotes digestion from oats and flax seeds.

- Healthy fats: Promote heart health from almonds and flax seeds.

- Antioxidants: Enhance overall health from cinnamon.

Sliced Pear with Ricotta Cheese

Ingredients:

- 1 pear, sliced
- 1/4 cup ricotta cheese
- 1 teaspoon honey
- 1/4 teaspoon cinnamon

Instructions:

1. Arrange pear slices on a plate.
2. Spoon ricotta cheese onto each slice.
3. Drizzle with honey and sprinkle with cinnamon.
4. Serve immediately.

Nutritional Values (per serving):

- Fiber: Promotes digestion from pear.
- Protein: Supports muscle repair from ricotta cheese.
- Vitamins: Enhance immune function from pear and cinnamon.

Edamame with Sea Salt

Ingredients:

- 1 cup edamame, shelled or in pods
- 1 teaspoon sea salt

Instructions:

1. Bring a pot of water to a boil. Add edamame and cook for 3-5 minutes until tender.
2. Drain and sprinkle with sea salt.
3. Serve immediately as a healthy snack.

Nutritional Values (per serving):

- Protein: Supports muscle repair from edamame.
- Fiber: Promotes digestion from edamame.
- Vitamins: Enhance immune function from edamame.

Mini Bell Peppers Stuffed with Tuna Salad

Ingredients:

- 6 mini bell peppers, halved and seeded
- 1 can tuna, drained
- 1/4 cup Greek yogurt
- 1 tablespoon lemon juice
- 1 celery stalk, finely chopped
- Salt and pepper to taste

Instructions:

1. In a bowl, combine drained tuna, Greek yogurt, lemon juice, finely chopped celery, salt, and pepper.
2. Stuff each mini bell pepper half with the tuna salad mixture.
3. Serve immediately.

Nutritional Values (per serving):

- Protein: Supports muscle repair from tuna.
- Fiber: Promotes digestion from mini bell peppers and celery.
- Vitamins: Enhance immune function from mini bell peppers.

Beet and Goat Cheese Salad

Ingredients:

- 2 beets, roasted and sliced
- 1/4 cup goat cheese, crumbled
- 1/4 cup walnuts, chopped
- 2 cups mixed greens
- 2 tablespoons balsamic vinaigrette

Instructions:

1. In a bowl, toss mixed greens with balsamic vinaigrette.
2. Top with roasted beet slices, crumbled goat cheese, and chopped walnuts.
3. Serve immediately as a fresh and healthy salad.

Nutritional Values (per serving):

- Vitamins: Enhance immune function from beets and mixed greens.
- Healthy fats: Promote heart health from walnuts and goat cheese.
- Protein: Supports muscle repair from goat cheese.

Smoked Salmon and Cream Cheese Cucumber Rolls

Ingredients:

- 1 cucumber, sliced thinly lengthwise
- 4 ounces smoked salmon
- 4 ounces cream cheese
- 1 tablespoon fresh dill, chopped

Instructions:

1. Spread a thin layer of cream cheese on each cucumber slice.
2. Top with smoked salmon and sprinkle with fresh dill.
3. Roll up each cucumber slice and secure with a toothpick if needed.
4. Serve immediately as a refreshing snack.

Nutritional Values (per serving):

- Omega-3 fatty acids: Promote heart health from smoked salmon.
- Healthy fats: Support brain function from cream cheese.
- Vitamins: Enhance immune function from cucumber and dill.

Chia Seed Pudding with Almond Milk and Berries

Ingredients:

- 1/4 cup chia seeds
- 1 cup almond milk
- 1 tablespoon honey
- 1/2 cup mixed berries

Instructions:

1. In a bowl, combine chia seeds, almond milk, and honey. Stir well.
2. Refrigerate for at least 4 hours or overnight, stirring occasionally.
3. Top with mixed berries before serving.

Nutritional Values (per serving):

- Omega-3 fatty acids: Promote heart health from chia seeds.

- Fiber: Promotes digestion from chia seeds and berries.

- Vitamins: Enhance immune function from berries.

5

56-DAY MEAL PLAN FOR METABOLIC CONFUSION DIET

Day 1 to Day 10

Day 1

- **Breakfast:** Greek Yogurt Parfait with Berries
- **Lunch:** Grilled Chicken Salad with Mixed Greens
- **Dinner:** Baked Cod with Lemon and Herbs
- **Snack:** Sliced Apple with Low-Fat Peanut Butter

Day 2

- **Breakfast:** Avocado Toast on Whole Grain Bread
- **Lunch:** Quinoa and Black Bean Stuffed Peppers
- **Dinner:** Turkey Meatballs with Spaghetti Squash
- **Snack:** Mixed Nuts and Raisins

Day 3

- **Breakfast:** Spinach and Mushroom Egg White Omelette
- **Lunch:** Vegetable Lentil Soup
- **Dinner:** Grilled Salmon with Steamed Asparagus
- **Snack:** Carrot and Celery Sticks with Hummus

Day 4

- **Breakfast:** Banana Oatmeal Pancakes
- **Lunch:** Tuna Salad Stuffed Avocado
- **Dinner:** Chicken and Broccoli Alfredo with Whole Wheat Pasta

- **Snack:** Greek Yogurt with Honey and Almonds

Day 5

- **Breakfast:** Smoothie Bowl with Papaya and Chia Seeds
- **Lunch:** Turkey and Hummus Wrap
- **Dinner:** Vegan Chili
- **Snack:** Baked Kale Chips

Day 6

- **Breakfast:** Baked Sweet Potato and Poached Eggs
- **Lunch:** Veggie and Goat Cheese Flatbread
- **Dinner:** Beef Stir Fry with Bell Peppers and Broccoli
- **Snack:** Cucumber Rounds with Dill Cream Cheese

Day 7

- **Breakfast:** Turkey Sausage and Bell Pepper Scramble
- **Lunch:** Grilled Shrimp and Mango Salad
- **Dinner:** Spaghetti with Turkey Meat Sauce
- **Snack:** Edamame with Sea Salt

Day 8

- **Breakfast:** Quinoa Porridge with Almonds and Apple

- **Lunch:** Grilled Vegetable and Hummus Tartine
- **Dinner:** Roast Chicken with Carrots and Potatoes
- **Snack:** Cottage Cheese with Sliced Tomato

Day 9

- **Breakfast:** Cottage Cheese with Pineapple and Mint
- **Lunch:** Sweet Potato and Black Bean Burrito
- **Dinner:** Ratatouille with Baked Polenta
- **Snack:** Fresh Fruit Salad

Day 10

- **Breakfast:** Vegan Blueberry Muffins
- **Lunch:** Chicken Caesar Salad with Low-Fat Dressing
- **Dinner:** Lemon Herb Roasted Chicken
- **Snack:** Guacamole with Whole Wheat Pita Chips

Day 11 to Day 20

Day 11

- **Breakfast:** Oatmeal with Banana and Almond Butter
- **Lunch:** Mediterranean Chickpea Salad

- **Dinner:** Grilled Steak with Mushroom Sauce
- **Snack:** Cherry Tomatoes with Mozzarella

Day 12

- **Breakfast:** Scrambled Eggs with Spinach and Feta
- **Lunch:** Curried Lentil Soup
- **Dinner:** Baked Tilapia with Tomato and Basil
- **Snack:** Apple Slices with Almond Butter

Day 13

- **Breakfast:** Berry Smoothie with Spinach and Flax Seeds
- **Lunch:** Quinoa Salad with Roasted Vegetables
- **Dinner:** Pork Chops with Apple Cider Glaze
- **Snack:** Greek Yogurt with Berries

Day 14

- **Breakfast:** Whole Grain Waffles with Fresh Berries
- **Lunch:** Turkey and Avocado Lettuce Wraps
- **Dinner:** Vegan Shepherd's Pie
- **Snack:** Roasted Pumpkin Seeds

Day 15

- **Breakfast:** Chia Seed Pudding with Almond Milk and Berries
- **Lunch:** Grilled Chicken and Quinoa Salad
- **Dinner:** Thai Green Curry with Shrimp
- **Snack:** Mixed Nuts

Day 16

- **Breakfast:** Egg Muffins with Spinach and Cheese
- **Lunch:** Tuna Salad with Mixed Greens
- **Dinner:** Slow Cooker Moroccan Chicken
- **Snack:** Carrot Sticks with Hummus

Day 17

- **Breakfast:** Mango and Spinach Smoothie
- **Lunch:** Caprese Salad with Balsamic Glaze
- **Dinner:** Herb-Crusted Rack of Lamb
- **Snack:** Cottage Cheese with Pineapple

Day 18

- **Breakfast:** Protein Pancakes with Blueberries

- **Lunch:** Black Bean and Corn Salad
- **Dinner:** Stuffed Chicken Breast with Spinach and Ricotta
- **Snack:** Fresh Fruit Salad

Day 19

- **Breakfast:** Greek Yogurt with Granola and Honey
- **Lunch:** Sweet Potato and Black Bean Chili
- **Dinner:** Balsamic Glazed Salmon
- **Snack:** Sliced Bell Peppers with Hummus

Day 20

- **Breakfast:** Avocado Smoothie with Banana and Spinach
- **Lunch:** Turkey and Veggie Wrap
- **Dinner:** Beef and Vegetable Kebabs
- **Snack:** Almonds and Dark Chocolate

Day 21 to Day 30

Day 21

- **Breakfast:** Smoothie Bowl with Mixed Berries and Chia Seeds
- **Lunch:** Grilled Chicken and Veggie Skewers
- **Dinner:** Seared Scallops with Cauliflower Puree
- **Snack:** Greek Yogurt with Honey

Day 22

- **Breakfast:** Scrambled Eggs with Avocado
- **Lunch:** Lentil Soup with Spinach
- **Dinner:** Vegetarian Paella
- **Snack:** Carrot and Celery Sticks with Hummus

Day 23

- **Breakfast:** Overnight Oats with Almond Butter and Banana
- **Lunch:** Turkey and Cheese Roll-Ups
- **Dinner:** Spaghetti Squash with Meatballs
- **Snack:** Mixed Nuts and Raisins

Day 24

- **Breakfast:** Berry and Spinach Smoothie

- **Lunch:** Grilled Vegetable Sandwich
- **Dinner:** Roasted Duck with Orange Sauce
- **Snack:** Apple Slices with Peanut Butter

Day 25

- **Breakfast:** Greek Yogurt with Berries and Honey
- **Lunch:** Chicken Caesar Salad
- **Dinner:** Grilled Mahi Mahi with Tropical Salsa
- **Snack:** Cottage Cheese with Pineapple

Day 26

- **Breakfast:** Spinach and Mushroom Omelette
- **Lunch:** Vegetable Stir Fry with Tofu
- **Dinner:** Grilled Salmon with Avocado Salsa
- **Snack:** Fresh Fruit Salad

Day 27

- **Breakfast:** Whole Grain Toast with Almond Butter and Banana
- **Lunch:** Tuna Salad Stuffed Avocado

- **Dinner:** Beef Stir Fry with Mixed Vegetables
- **Snack:** Sliced Cucumber with Hummus

Day 28

- **Breakfast:** Smoothie Bowl with Papaya and Chia Seeds
- **Lunch:** Turkey and Hummus Wrap
- **Dinner:** Baked Falafel with Tzatziki Sauce
- **Snack:** Kale Chips

Day 29

- **Breakfast:** Cottage Cheese with Sliced Peaches and Honey
- **Lunch:** Turkey Sausage and Bell Pepper Scramble
- **Dinner:** Baked Tilapia with Tomato and Basil
- **Snack:** Carrot and Celery Sticks with Hummus

Day 30

- **Breakfast:** Chia Seed Pudding with Almond Milk and Berries
- **Lunch:** Grilled Chicken Salad with Mixed Greens
- **Dinner:** Pork Tenderloin with Applesauce
- **Snack:** Mixed Nuts and Raisins

Day 31 to Day 40

Day 31

- **Breakfast:** Greek Yogurt with Honey and Walnuts
- **Lunch:** Grilled Shrimp and Mango Salad
- **Dinner:** Stuffed Chicken Breast with Spinach and Ricotta
- **Snack:** Sliced Apple with Almond Butter

Day 32

- **Breakfast:** Avocado Toast on Whole Grain Bread
- **Lunch:** Quinoa and Black Bean Salad
- **Dinner:** Turkey Meatballs with Spaghetti Squash
- **Snack:** Cottage Cheese with Pineapple

Day 33

- **Breakfast:** Smoothie Bowl with Spinach and Banana
- **Lunch:** Vegetable Lentil Soup
- **Dinner:** Grilled Salmon with Steamed Asparagus

- **Snack:** Carrot and Celery Sticks with Hummus

Day 34

- **Breakfast:** Oatmeal with Blueberries and Almonds
- **Lunch:** Tuna Salad with Mixed Greens
- **Dinner:** Chicken and Broccoli Alfredo with Whole Wheat Pasta
- **Snack:** Greek Yogurt with Honey and Almonds

Day 35

- **Breakfast:** Protein-Packed Smoothie with Chia Seeds
- **Lunch:** Turkey and Hummus Wrap
- **Dinner:** Vegan Chili
- **Snack:** Baked Kale Chips

Day 36

- **Breakfast:** Baked Sweet Potato and Poached Eggs
- **Lunch:** Veggie and Goat Cheese Flatbread
- **Dinner:** Beef Stir Fry with Bell Peppers and Broccoli
- **Snack:** Cucumber Rounds with Dill Cream Cheese

Day 37

- **Breakfast:** Turkey Sausage and Bell Pepper Scramble
- **Lunch:** Grilled Shrimp and Mango Salad
- **Dinner:** Spaghetti with Turkey Meat Sauce
- **Snack:** Edamame with Sea Salt

Day 38

- **Breakfast:** Quinoa Porridge with Almonds and Apple
- **Lunch:** Grilled Vegetable and Hummus Tartine
- **Dinner:** Roast Chicken with Carrots and Potatoes
- **Snack:** Cottage Cheese with Sliced Tomato

Day 39

- **Breakfast:** Cottage Cheese with Pineapple and Mint
- **Lunch:** Sweet Potato and Black Bean Burrito
- **Dinner:** Ratatouille with Baked Polenta
- **Snack:** Fresh Fruit Salad

Day 40

- **Breakfast:** Vegan Blueberry Muffins
- **Lunch:** Chicken Caesar Salad with Low-Fat Dressing

- **Dinner:** Lemon Herb Roasted Chicken
- **Snack:** Guacamole with Whole Wheat Pita Chips

Day 41 to Day 50

Day 41

- **Breakfast:** Greek Yogurt Parfait with Berries
- **Lunch:** Grilled Chicken Salad with Mixed Greens
- **Dinner:** Baked Cod with Lemon and Herbs
- **Snack:** Sliced Apple with Low-Fat Peanut Butter

Day 42

- **Breakfast:** Avocado Toast on Whole Grain Bread
- **Lunch:** Quinoa and Black Bean Stuffed Peppers
- **Dinner:** Turkey Meatballs with Spaghetti Squash
- **Snack:** Mixed Nuts and Raisins

Day 43

- **Breakfast:** Spinach and Mushroom Egg White Omelette
- **Lunch:** Vegetable Lentil Soup
- **Dinner:** Grilled Salmon with Steamed Asparagus

- **Snack:** Carrot and Celery Sticks with Hummus

Day 44

- **Breakfast:** Banana Oatmeal Pancakes
- **Lunch:** Tuna Salad Stuffed Avocado
- **Dinner:** Chicken and Broccoli Alfredo with Whole Wheat Pasta
- **Snack:** Greek Yogurt with Honey and Almonds

Day 45

- **Breakfast:** Smoothie Bowl with Papaya and Chia Seeds
- **Lunch:** Turkey and Hummus Wrap
- **Dinner:** Vegan Chili
- **Snack:** Baked Kale Chips

Day 46

- **Breakfast:** Baked Sweet Potato and Poached Eggs
- **Lunch:** Veggie and Goat Cheese Flatbread
- **Dinner:** Beef Stir Fry with Bell Peppers and Broccoli

- **Snack:** Cucumber Rounds with Dill Cream Cheese

Day 47

- **Breakfast:** Turkey Sausage and Bell Pepper Scramble
- **Lunch:** Grilled Shrimp and Mango Salad
- **Dinner:** Spaghetti with Turkey Meat Sauce
- **Snack:** Edamame with Sea Salt

Day 48

- **Breakfast:** Quinoa Porridge with Almonds and Apple
- **Lunch:** Grilled Vegetable and Hummus Tartine
- **Dinner:** Roast Chicken with Carrots and Potatoes
- **Snack:** Cottage Cheese with Sliced Tomato

Day 49

- **Breakfast:** Cottage Cheese with Pineapple and Mint
- **Lunch:** Sweet Potato and Black Bean Burrito
- **Dinner:** Ratatouille with Baked Polenta
- **Snack:** Fresh Fruit Salad

Day 50

- **Breakfast:** Vegan Blueberry Muffins
- **Lunch:** Chicken Caesar Salad with Low-Fat Dressing
- **Dinner:** Lemon Herb Roasted Chicken
- **Snack:** Guacamole with Whole Wheat Pita Chips

Day 51 to Day 56

Day 51

- **Breakfast:** Greek Yogurt Parfait with Berries
- **Lunch:** Grilled Chicken Salad with Mixed Greens
- **Dinner:** Baked Cod with Lemon and Herbs
- **Snack:** Sliced Apple with Low-Fat Peanut Butter

Day 52

- **Breakfast:** Avocado Toast on Whole Grain Bread
- **Lunch:** Quinoa and Black Bean Stuffed Peppers
- **Dinner:** Turkey Meatballs with Spaghetti Squash
- **Snack:** Mixed Nuts and Raisins

Day 53

- **Breakfast:** Spinach and Mushroom Egg White Omelette
- **Lunch:** Vegetable Lentil Soup
- **Dinner:** Grilled Salmon with Steamed Asparagus
- **Snack:** Carrot and Celery Sticks with Hummus

Day 54

- **Breakfast:** Banana Oatmeal Pancakes
- **Lunch:** Tuna Salad Stuffed Avocado
- **Dinner:** Chicken and Broccoli Alfredo with Whole Wheat Pasta
- **Snack:** Greek Yogurt with Honey and Almonds

Day 55

- **Breakfast:** Smoothie Bowl with Papaya and Chia Seeds
- **Lunch:** Turkey and Hummus Wrap
- **Dinner:** Vegan Chili
- **Snack:** Baked Kale Chips

Day 56

- **Breakfast:** Baked Sweet Potato and Poached Eggs

- **Lunch:** Veggie and Goat Cheese Flatbread

- **Dinner:** Beef Stir Fry with Bell Peppers and Broccoli

- **Snack:** Cucumber Rounds with Dill Cream Cheese

This 56-day meal plan provides a balanced and varied diet, ensuring that you get a wide range of nutrients from different food sources. Each day includes a nutritious breakfast, lunch, dinner, and a healthy snack to keep you energized and satisfied. Enjoy these meals and feel the positive impact on your health and well-being!

SCAN THE QR CODE AND IMMEDIATELY ACCESS YOUR 3 SPECIAL BONUSES IN DIGITAL FORMAT!

🔥 **Bonus 1: Dining Out Without Derailing Your Diet**

🔥 **Bonus 2: Recognizing Your Body Type**

🔥 **Bonus 3: Weekly Grocery Planner**

Made in United States
Orlando, FL
28 November 2024

54585444R00052